Guide

TO THE MUSÉE RODIN

Collections

ÉDITIONS DU MUSÉE RODIN

Note to the reader
Except when otherwise mentioned, the works in the Musée Rodin presented in this book came from the donation Rodin made to France in 1916.

The Musée Rodin owns the copyright of the Alexis and Georges Rudier foundries, Paris.

To facilitate finding the description of a specific work, the entry number is indicated in brackets each time it is mentioned, e.g. *The Kiss* (33).

The titles of Rodin's works include the definite article when this is part of the title. The definite article thus appears in italics and starts with a capital letter, even in the middle of a sentence, e.g. "Designed for *The Gates of Hell*, circa 1885."

All the dimensions of the works in this guide are indicated in centimetres.

The sources of some of the quotations are cited in brackets: the name of the author, followed by a date [e.g. (Rilke, 1908)]. The reader may then refer to the bibliography at the end of the book, where the references are listed according to the author's name and the year.

The letters in the "Archives" section are transcribed as they were written, with any grammatical, spelling and syntactic mistakes.

The initials at the bottom of the entries and introductory texts refer to the following authors:
François Blanchetière (F.B.)
Sylvester Engbrox (S.E.)
Bénédicte Garnier (B.G.)
Nadine Lehni (N.L.)
Aline Magnien (A.M.)
Hélène Marraud (H.M.)
Véronique Mattiussi (V.M.)
Aurore Méchain (Au.M.)
Hélène Pinet (H.P.)

The intials SNBA stand for Société nationale des Beaux-Arts.

Published by the Musée Rodin

Department Head of the collections
Christine Lancestremère
Heritage Curator-in-Chief

Editor: Jean-Baptiste Chantoiseau

Photo Agency: Jérôme Manoukian
and Pauline Hisbacq

Translation: Pamela Hargreaves

Graphic design and layout: Pierre Finot

Photoengraving: MCP – Groupe Jouve
and Planète Couleurs

Printed by Fabrikant, Le Mans

Communication: Clémence Goldberger
and Anaïs Izard

Distributed by the Musée Rodin
19, boulevard des Invalides
75007 Paris
servcom@musee-rodin.fr
www.musee-rodin.fr

Cover illustration: *I Am Beautiful* (29)
© Musée Rodin, photo Christian Baraja.

© Musée Rodin, Paris, 2018
1ˢᵗ edition: 2008
All translation, reproduction and
adaptation rights reserved worldwide
ISBN 978-2-35377-009-0

Guide
TO THE MUSÉE RODIN
Collections

Under the general editorship of
Catherine CHEVILLOT
Heritage Curator
Director of the Musée Rodin

and
Aline MAGNIEN
Heritage Curator-in-Chief

François BLANCHETIÈRE
Heritage Curator

Sylvester ENGBROX
Researcher

Bénédicte GARNIER
Coordinator of scientific activities for Rodin
and Meudon collection

Nadine LEHNI
Heritage Curator-in-Chief,
with the assistance of Aurore MÉCHAIN

Hélène MARRAUD
Assistant Curator in charge of Sculpture

Véronique MATTIUSSI
Scientific Manager in charge of Historic Archives,
Assistant to the Department Head of Research, Documentation,
Library and Archives

Hélène PINET
Head of Research, Documentation,
Library and Archives

ÉDITIONS DU MUSÉE RODIN, 2018

The Musée Rodin introduces visitors to not only the works but also the world of France's leading sculptor of the period 1880-1910. Thanks to the donations that he made to the French State in 1916, first and foremost Auguste Rodin (1840-1917) enabled his entire body of work to be preserved, i.e. some 15,000 terracottas, plasters, marbles, bronzes and drawings. Yet he donated far more than that, namely his personal collections – some 6,500 pieces – particularly rich in Egyptian, Greek and Roman antiquities; approximately 200 paintings, some by him as well as an unusual collection by his contemporaries and friends; his archives and photographs; and, lastly, his estate in Meudon, the second Musée Rodin, still much lesser known, despite meaning as much to Rodin as Giverny did to Monet.

In 1911, to house these works, the State purchased the mansion known as the Hôtel Biron, which Rodin had occupied as a tenant at Rilke's suggestion since 1908. The rooms, under partial renovation from 2012 to 2015, enable visitors to follow the artist's career and aesthetic development, from the early decorative stage of the 1860s to his more symbolist investigations at the end of his life, via an unparalleled expressionism exploring human passions that gave birth to *The Gates of Hell* (1880-90). The immense wealth of the collection makes it possible to show the progression of Rodin's experimental and creative processes throughout his life.

But this *Guide to the Collections* also hopes to serve as a sort of toolbox, helping visitors to construct their own itinerary. For there are several alternatives to a chronological tour: the dialogue between the Hôtel Biron and its gardens has always been an extraordinary asset, which no doubt was a major factor in Rodin's decision to move here. Visitors may thus simply let themselves be surprised by the play of

View of the Hôtel Biron, the south façade seen from the gardens of the Musée Rodin.

light on the forms and materials; or be charmed by the unexpected interaction between individual works; and discover the echo effect between drawings and models inside the museum and the bronzes erected outside. In short, through the alchemy of the site and works, visitors may learn or learn anew to see how forms in space give rise to multiple ways of looking and perceiving.

And so I invite the public to return to discover or rediscover the Hôtel Biron which reopened in November 2015 after three-and-a-half-years of work: the fully refurbished rooms and updated exhibition design present a much richer itinerary, including numerous works previously held in storage, as well as a gallery in which drawings, photographs and archival documents will be displayed according to a rota system.

Lastly, I particularly urge visitors to make a detour via Meudon: home to Rodin from 1893 until the time of his death, it was also the place where he created, met people, exchanged ideas and worked. He used the Hôtel Biron as a showroom where he received his clients, but

Meudon was his secret garden. His residence, the "Villa des Brillants", the museum that houses numerous original plaster models, built thanks to the sculptor's American patron Jules Mastbaum (1872–1926), who also founded the Rodin Museum in Philadelphia, and the tomb in which Rodin wanted to be buried with his wife, watched over by *The Thinker*, all attest to this intimate atmosphere. The sculptor liked to gather his thoughts in the early morning mist in the grounds stretching over three hectares and overlooking the Seine Valley.

All the museum personnel hope visitors will enjoy discovering or rediscovering Rodin and his two museums.

Catherine CHEVILLOT
Heritage curator
Director of the Musée Rodin

Fig. 1
Anonymous, *Portrait of Rodin wearing
a Plaster-Splattered Jacket*, 1880, albumen
print, Ph. 311.

Véronique MATTIUSSI

The life and work of Auguste Rodin

An illustrious artist in his own lifetime, Auguste Rodin still epitomizes the genius of sculpture today (fig. 1). He was born on 12 November 1840, in the Rue de l'Arbalète, in a poor but lively district of Paris' 12th *arrondissement* (present-day 5th).

As a boy from a modest family, he was easily distracted, remained a lack-lustre pupil and received a mediocre education. However, his real gift for drawing persuaded his father to allow him, from the age of 14, to attend the *École Impériale Spéciale de Dessin et de Mathématiques*, called the "Petite École" to distinguish it from the *École des Beaux-Arts*. His career as an artist got off to a slow start, since he failed the entrance examination to the *École des Beaux-Arts* three times in a row, which meant that all his hopes of winning the prestigious *Prix de Rome* were dashed.

To support his family, Rodin, who, at this time, was more of an assistant than a creative artist, worked for ornamentalists and decorative sculptors. He was employed by Ernest Carrier-Belleuse, with whom he went to Belgium, before forming a partnership with Antoine-Joseph Van Rasbourgh. In 1875, while still unknown, Rodin realized a youthful dream by making an eagerly-planned visit to Italy, a compulsory step in any artistic career. His discovery of Michelangelo made a huge impact on him.

His career was punctuated by scandals. In 1877, he was accused of using a life cast for his statue *The Age of Bronze* (6), when he exhibited it in Brussels. Yet this first *cause célèbre* and first masterpiece helped establish his reputation as a sculptor.

Throughout his working life, he was awarded major commissions such as *The Burghers of Calais* (20-25), the *Monument to Victor Hugo* (39-40) and his statue of *Balzac* (50-52, 65), which caused so much controversy that it was refused by the *Société des Gens de Lettres*, when it was shown – at the same time as *The Kiss* (33) – at the Salon in 1898 (fig. 2). Slandered by some, adulated by others, Rodin worked unremittingly.

In 1880, he received the commission for a portal for a future Museum of Decorative Arts: *The Gates of Hell* (11-14), inspired by Dante's *Divine Comedy*. On the tympanum sat the Poet, sorrowfully contemplating the crowd of damned souls beneath him. An enlarged version of *The Thinker* (68) was erected outside the Panthéon, in Paris, in 1906, and went on to become a universal icon (fig. 3). Rodin worked on these *Gates* all his life, endlessly drawing on this repertory of forms to create new sculptures.

Bodily movements, repetition or combinations of figures and fragmentation, which sacrificed detail to better express the essential, were all areas in which the pioneering Rodin boldly experimented.

Fig. 2
Anonymous,
"*Monument
to Balzac*" at the
Salon de la SNBA,
1898, aristotype
print, Ph. 267.

In 1882, he was entranced by the fiery temperament and outstanding talent of his new pupil, Camille Claudel, who later became his assistant, mistress and muse.

Rodin left Paris in 1893 to live in Meudon, where he began a new career as a collector. In record time, he assembled a vast number of objects from different periods and civilizations, purchased from art dealers, at auction sales or even from private individuals.

Rodin was a hard-working man who lived a simple, often even contemplative life, which was later replaced by a society lifestyle full of amorous adventures that continued to be widely talked about.

In 1900, there was a decisive turning-point in his career, when he mounted an independent exhibition of his works at the *Pavillon de*

l'Alma, coinciding with the Paris *Exposition Universelle*. Finally recognized and financially secure, the sculptor was showered with tributes and invited to all sorts of celebrations.

Every day, he travelled from Meudon to his studio in the Rue de l'Université, then, from 1908 onwards, to the Hôtel Biron, where he received admirers, curious visitors and collectors. During the last years of his life, this was where he devoted more time to drawing than modelling.

Assisted by his loyal friends, Rodin then fought his final battle: to establish his own museum.

Fig 3
Marcel Hutin,
*Unveiling
of "The Thinker"
outside the
Panthéon*, Paris,
21 April 1906,
gelatin-silver print,
Ph. 2087.

Thus began a long and complex series of negotiations with the French state. In the end, after much heated debate, caused either out of fear of creating a regrettable precedent or out of hostility towards the artist – "the decadent", "the subversive" – and his immoral works, Rodin suggested donating his entire collections to the French nation in three stages (1 April, 13 September, 25 October 1916). On 24 December 1916, in the middle of World War I, the Chamber of Deputies, then the Senate, accepted the donation, and the National Assembly voted in the establishment of the Musée Rodin in the Hôtel Biron.

Shortly after having married his lifelong companion, Rose Beuret, Rodin died on 17 November 1917, in his villa in Meudon, where he was buried.

Two years later, on 4 August 1919, after delays caused by the war, the Musée Rodin opened its doors to the public.

V. M.

Fig. 1
C. Lemery,
Rodin Reading,
22 April 1912,
aristotype,
Ph.196.

François BLANCHETIÈRE

Rodin at the Hôtel Biron and Meudon

In 1908, the Austrian poet Rainer Maria Rilke, who had previously worked as Rodin's secretary, invited the sculptor to come and admire the office he then occupied at the Hôtel Biron. "Out of the window," he wrote, "from time to time, one can see innocent rabbits jumping through the trelliswork, as in an ancient tapestry," (Rilke, 1908). The garden of this handsome private mansion, built between 1728 and 1730 by the architect Jean Aubert for the wealthy financier Abraham Peyrenc de Moras, had, in fact, almost run wild, after several decades of neglect.

Yet it had been one of the most beautiful gardens in Paris during the second half of the 18th century, when owned by the Maréchal de Biron, from whom the mansion took its name. After the latter's death, in 1788, it became home to a series of residents, including the Russian ambassador and the apostolic nuncio. In 1820, the order of the Ladies of the Sacred Heart purchased the mansion to be used as an educational institution for girls. The sisters renovated the garden and had several auxiliary buildings constructed, including a neo-Gothic chapel (present-day temporary exhibition room) and a large boarding school (present-day Lycée Victor Duruy). They sold the mansion's interior decoration – wrought ironwork, woodwork, mirrors, overdoor paintings – some of which have since been repurchased or reconstructed by the museum. In the late 19th century, most of the grounds served as a kitchen garden, an orchard or pastureland, while numerous oratories lined the paths where the trees had grown very tall. The sisters were evicted in 1904, when the law forbidding religious congregations to be involved in education came into force.

This was followed by a period of uncertainty: should the mansion be demolished and the land divided up into plots or should the handsome group of buildings be preserved? While this was being decided, the rooms of the different buildings were rented out and several artists moved in: the dancer Isadora Duncan opened her school of dance in a gallery overlooking the main courtyard; Matisse had a studio in the boarding school; Rodin occupied a suite of rooms on the ground floor of the mansion (fig. 1). He never lived there, preferring to use these prestigious premises to receive his numerous admirers, having brought some of his furniture and some of the pieces from his collection to show people at the same time as his own works. Through his powerful political relations, he managed to postpone the sale of the Hôtel Biron, which was envisaged several times from 1909 onwards,

and then ensure that the great project of his final years – the founding of his museum – would be accepted.

Rodin's real home was, in fact, the *Villa des Brillants*, in Meudon (figs. 2-3). After renting it for two years, he purchased it in 1895. In this modest residence, he led a quiet life with Rose Beuret. The pavilion that had housed his

Fig. 2
Anonymous,
*The Villa
des Brillants and the
Pavillon de l'Alma,
seen from the south,*
after 1901,
gelatin–silver print,
Ph. 1941.

solo exhibition in 1900 was reconstructed in the garden at his request. He used it as a studio and for storing his vast collections of plasters, on which he continued to work. This temporary structure was replaced in 1930 by the present museum building, which is open to the public, as is the villa and the garden in which the tomb of the sculptor and his wife can be found, beneath a large bronze cast of *The Thinker* **(68)**.

F. B.

Fig. 3
Frank Bal, *Rodin
seated admidst his
collection*, circa 1905,
gelatin-silver print,
Ph. 7004.

1. THE WORKS OF RODIN

François BLANCHETIÈRE, *Aline* MAGNIEN, *Hélène* MARRAUD

Sculptures

Rodin was an extraordinary creative artist and a prolific worker. After attending the "Petite École", he worked in the studio of the ornamentalist Albert-Ernest Carrier-Belleuse, first in Paris, then in Brussels, where his skill in handling decorative subjects fashionable in the 18th century became apparent. His discovery of Michelangelo, during a visit to Italy in 1875-76, was a decisive moment in his career. Rodin would, in turn, break new ground in sculpture, paving the way for 20th-century art, by introducing methods and techniques that were central to his own artistic aesthetics.

Having completed *The Age of Bronze* (6) and *Saint John the Baptist* (9), which attest to his mastery of the human figure, he began, in the course of the 1890s, to fragment and mutilate his nudes to render them more forceful and expressive, retaining only what he considered essential: *The Walking Man* (73) and *Meditation* (48). His fondness for fragmentary sculpture asserted itself, guided by the example of ancient works that have most frequently survived in this condition. But for Rodin, they formed a whole; nothing was missing from them.

At the same time, he did not consider it beneath him to work as a portraitist, and, from the early stages of his career, made numerous busts: portraits of his friends and contemporaries, people close to him, famous men, like *Victor Hugo* (18) and *Clemenceau* (85), or, especially after 1900, women friends and socialites. What he always sought to capture was their personality, the sitter's most intimate side, the inner truth that confers an eternal quality upon a portrait.

Different commissions for monuments, to which he always responded enthusiastically and which provided him with financial security, punctuated the sculptor's career (from 1880 to 1916) and traced the development of his art and research: Monuments to *The Burghers of Calais* (20-25), *Bastien-Lepage* and *Claude Lorrain*. But several remained

The Kiss (33), detail.

19

unfinished or were refused: *The Gates of Hell* (**11-14**), *Victor Hugo* (**39-40**), *Balzac* (**50-52, 65**) and *Whistler* (**79**). Apart from the vicissitudes of a commission, the rejected monuments underline the gap between the client's idea and the project designed by the sculptor.

After 1900, a date that marked a turning-point in Rodin's career, owing to the major retrospective of his work held at the *Pavillon de l'Alma*, Paris, independently of the *Exposition Universelle*, the sculptor focused more on exploiting his existing works than on creating new ones. Various processes, including enlargement or reduction, repetition and assemblage, and the translation into other media like glass paste or stoneware, enabled him to apply a new approach to his previous works. The enlargement of a full figure, or of one of its parts (torso, head), modified the way in which the original work was perceived and granted it a different autonomy. By using two or more casts of the same figure, he introduced mirror effects into sculpture, as in *The Three Shades* (**30**). By making multiple casts of pre-existing works, notably *bozzetti* – the tiny sculptural studies of arms, heads and hands – he obtained a repertory of forms from which he could borrow as often as he wanted (**38**). Initially an industrial process, mass production thus became a means of creation for Rodin: it enabled him to bring the hand and the mind closer together, to unite the form and the idea, shortening the creative act in a swifter, more spontaneous gesture.

He then proceeded to play a veritable game of reconstruction. He constantly took his works apart, put them back together, assembling limbs, torsos and figures with each other, sometimes incorporating ancient vases from his collections into his compositions, using them as receptacles for his tiny nudes (**59-60**). His only concern was the

Fugit Amor (35),
detail.

arrangement of forms in space. But his oeuvre would never have attained the scale with which we are familiar today had he not had such a well-organized studio, which in 1900, employed about 50 people – practitioners, mould-makers, assistants and pupils, some of whom went on to make their own careers (Jules Desbois, Antoine Bourdelle, Camille Claudel).

H. M.

1

Father Eymard

1863

Bronze, cast by Alexis Rudier, 1917
H. 59.3 cm; W. 29 cm; D. 29.2 cm
S. 972

In 1856, Father Pierre-Julien Eymard (1811-68) founded the Brotherhood of the Holy Sacrament, in which Rodin took refuge, in late December 1862, three weeks after the death of his sister, Maria.

Probably commenced in February 1863, the bust of this saintly man (the process of his canonization would be concluded in 1962) was influenced by the work of David d'Angers. The herm-like form confers a certain abstract quality upon it, counterbalanced by the attention paid to the treatment of the clothes and hair. This thick, unruly head of hair accentuates the intensity of his gaze and the spirituality of the face with prominent cheekbones and thin, straight nose. The lively modelling is full of light and shadow. Father Eymard was not only similar in spiritual outlook to Jean-Marie Vianney (1786-1859), the curate of Ars, but also resembled him physically: he had the same piercing gaze, ascetic leanness and thick mass of hair. The cult and iconography of the curate of Ars were already very widespread.

The subject's personality is emphasized by the scroll placed on his chest, bearing a fragment of Eymard's prayer: "O Sacrament Most Holy, O Sacrament Divine, all praise and all thanksgiving be every moment thine."

A. M.

Trained by Carrier-Belleuse, who drew his inspiration from the 18th century, Rodin produced works showing the influence of Second Empire trends. The economic advantages of this essentially decorative production were far from negligible, but Rodin succeeded in infusing these works with his own dynamic sense of modelling.

Even if distinctive features were discreetly added, in general these heads of young women all had a somewhat conventional appearance, which conferred a primarily ornamental role upon them. Represented with seasonal flowers – roses, lilacs – or fruit – grapes, vine leaves and tendrils – in their hair, most of them date from the time known as the "Belgian" period.

A. M.

2

Young Girl with Flowers in her Hair

1870

Terracotta
H. 49.5 cm; W. 34 cm; D. 24 cm
S. 211

3

Ixelles Idyll

Circa 1875

Bronze, lost wax cast, probably by Eugène
Gonon, 1885
H. 53 cm; W. 41 cm; D. 41.5 cm
Purchased by the museum in 1956
S. 978

This decorative group takes its name from the marble version, dated 1884, now in the Musée d'Ixelles, near Brussels. Designed circa 1875, when Rodin was living in Belgium, it has no other subject but the innocent happiness its suggests: a cherub and a young child, both plump and chubby-cheeked, are embracing each other on a wide plinth scattered with flowers. The delicacy of the details of the present bronze is highlighted by the excellent quality of the cast, made in 1885 using the lost-wax process revived by Eugène Gonon. Still showing the influence of Carrier-Belleuse, *Ixelles Idyll* is a good example of the works Rodin produced in a decorative style popular in the 18th century, which returned to fashion under the Second Empire. The gaiety of the subject and the liveliness of Rodin's handling gave rise to several comparisons with Clodion (1738-1814), who, a century earlier, had made numerous charming sculptures representing children at play.

F. B.

This work, executed circa 1863, has a long history. The original plaster bust froze and the back of the head fell off. Rodin submitted the remaining mask to the Salon of 1865, but without success. The marble, carved by Léon Fourquet, dating from the winter of 1874-75, however, was accepted at the Salon of 1875.

The sitter for the bust, which began as a simple portrait, was an elderly workman from the Saint-Marcel district of Paris, who went by the name of "Bibi". By emphasizing certain features – the broken nose, the deep lines, the style of the beard – Rodin established a parallel between this face and Michelangelo's, and thus the individual portrait dissolved into an archetype. The way in which the bust is cut, its "philosophical" nudity and the classical-style fillet in the hair heighten the impression of a work that is no longer entirely an individual portrait, but one that, by accentuating certain distinctive features, amalgamates general characteristics attributed to the philospher and the artist.

In many respects, this early portrait by Rodin epitomizes the sculptor's working method and, above all, his concept of portraiture.

A. M.

4

Man with the Broken Nose

1863-1875

Marble
H. 56.8 cm; W. 41.5 cm; D. 23.9 cm
S. 974

5

ALBERT-ERNEST CARRIER-BELLEUSE
(1824-1887) AND AUGUSTE RODIN

Pedestal of the Titans

1870-1882?

Glazed ceramic,
Manufacture de Choisy-le-Roi?
H. 39 cm; W. 37 cm; D. 36 cm
Purchased by the museum, 2004
S. 6739

On completing his studies at the art school known as the "Petite École", Rodin spent several years working for various masters, the most important of whom was Albert-Ernest Carrier-Belleuse, who made good use of his remarkable modelling skills. This fashionable sculptor, famous for his prolific decorative output, ran an extremely well-organized studio, which enabled him to handle all the numerous commissions he received. Rodin modelled the male figures adorning this pedestal designed by his master – a support for a decorative vase to be cast in a limited edition.

The vigorous musculature of the Titans portrayed here in twisting poses shows Rodin's admiration for Michelangelo. Influenced by the works of the great Italian sculptor, Rodin already managed to combine his keen observation of the anatomy with a remarkable sense of exaggeration in the details that heightened the expression of his figures. The bodies, here, have a tormented force entirely in keeping with the depiction of the mythological Titans, the primitive giants vanquished by the gods of Olympus.

F. B.

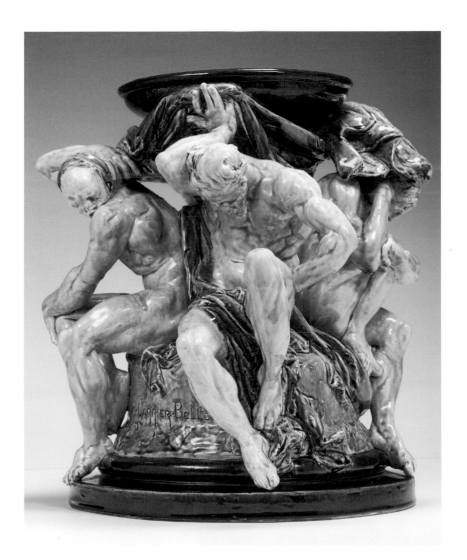

Made in Brussels, this figure, one of Rodin's most famous works, attests to the sculptor's masterly skill and his attention to living nature that informs the pose and the modelling. A young Belgian soldier, Auguste Ney, was the model for this statue devoid of any element that would shed light on the subject's identity. The untitled work was exhibited at the *Cercle Artistique*, Brussels, in 1877, then, entitled *The Age of Bronze*, at the Salon in Paris, where it caused a scandal.

Also known as *The Awakening Man* or *The Vanquished One*, the statue recalls one of the early ages of mankind. There was originally a spear in the left hand, as is shown in a photograph by Gaudenzio Marconi (140), but Rodin decided to suppress the weapon so as to free the arm of any attribute and infuse the gesture with a new liberality.

Accused of having used a life cast of his sitter, when the statue was shown in Paris, Rodin had to prove that the quality of his sculpture's modelling came from a thorough study of profiles, not from a life cast. His critics eventually recognized that the sculptor was innocent of any trickery. The scandal, however, did draw attention to Rodin and earned him the commission for *The Gates of Hell* in 1880 (11–14).

H. M.

6

The Age of Bronze

1877

Bronze, cast by Alexis Rudier,
before 1916
H. 180.5 cm; W. 68.5 cm; D. 54.5 cm
S. 986

7

J. Danielli

1878

Bronze, cast by François Rudier, 1883
H. 44 cm; W. 27.5 cm; D. 28.8 cm
Purchased by the Musée Rodin, 1995
S. 6669

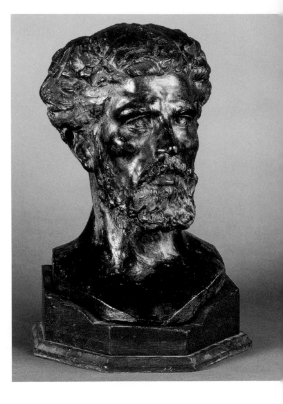

This is probably one of the first portraits Rodin made on his return to Paris in 1877. J. Danielli, whose identity remains uncertain, but who was possibly related to Bassano Danielli (1854-1923), a sculptor active in Milan, made his living from "Hardening, Metallization and Artistic Decoration of Plaster". He worked on several occasions for Rodin or his circle of acquaintances. In 1879, he "galvanized" the plaster bust of *Saint John the Baptist* (9). Then, in 1895, he used the same process on Camille Claudel's *Sakuntala*, when she donated it to the museum in Châteauroux.

Danielli's bust was one of the numerous portraits of friends or people close to him that Rodin made for practical reasons or out of affection. The sculptor no doubt wanted to capture the vitality and creativity of Danielli's bubbling personality in the movement of his wavy hair, which accentuates the effect of closeness and warmth emanating from this bust with lively modelling.

A. M.

8

Bellona

1879

Bronze, cast by Alexis Rudier, 1917?
H. 80 cm (with base 103 cm);
W. 53.5 cm; D. 41 cm
Possibly the seventh cast, made
in September 1917, gift of Rodin
"to Mme Rodin for Auguste Beuret"
and immediately sold by Beuret;
bequest of Mme Eugène Rudier,
1957.
S. 476

In 1879, Rodin took part in a competition to design a *Monument to the Republic*, which would adorn the new town hall in Paris' 8th *arrondissement*.

Possibly inspired by his companion Rose Beuret in a fit of anger, the bust initially appeared under the names of warrior heroines such as *Clorinda*, *Hippolyta*, and then *Bellona*, the Roman goddess of war, considered by some to be the wife of Mars, and who here became the personification of the Republic. Rodin placed a Renaissance-style helmet on her head instead of the Phrygian cap specified in the competition rules.

The result was a sullen, belligerent, somewhat rebellious Republic, totally out of keeping with the image the French government wanted to project, evoking instead a nation thirsting for revenge after its defeat by the Prussians in 1870.

However, the bust was much admired by artists like Dubois, Falguière, Carrier-Belleuse and Chapu, who recognized the sculptor's talent as a modeller and his power of expression.

Rodin lost the competition, but the bust may be regarded as one of his strongest works.

H. M.

9

Saint John the Baptist

1880

Bronze, cast by Alexis Rudier, 1915?
H. 203 cm; W. 71.7 cm; D. 119.5 cm
S. 999

Like *The Age of Bronze* (6), this figure is portrayed without the usual attributes that helped identify the subject: only the gesture seemingly suspended in space remains.

Rodin himself described how the idea for this figure had been suggested to him by an Italian peasant from the Abruzzi called Pignatelli, who came to offer him his services as a model: "As soon as I saw him, I was filled with admiration; this rough, hairy man expressed violence in his bearing... yet also the mystical character of his race. I immediately thought of a Saint John the Baptist, in other words, a man of nature, a visionary, a believer, a precursor who came to announce one greater than himself. The peasant undressed, climbed onto the revolving stand as if he had never posed before; he planted himself firmly on his feet, head up, torso straight, at the same time putting his weight on both legs, open like a compass. The movement was so right, so straightforward and so true that I cried: 'But it's a man walking!' I immediately resolved to model what I had seen." (Dujardin-Beaumetz, 1913).

H. M.

10

Saigon Vase,
"Limbo and the Sirens"

1887, 1934 edition

Porcelain, Manufacture Nationale
de Sèvres
H. 24.7 cm; W. 13.3 cm; D. 13.3 cm
Gift of Eugène Rudier in 1945
S. 2415

Rodin worked for the Sèvres Porcelain Factory from 1879 and 1882, then continued on an occasional basis until the end of the 1880s. Carrier-Belleuse, appointed artistic director in 1875 with the task of reviving production, called upon the services of four sculptors whom he most valued for their modelling skills. Rodin was one of the best of them. On the vases with novel forms designed by Carrier-Belleuse, his job was to apply decorative motifs in very light relief, veritable feats of skill halfway between sculpture and drawing.

The themes represented on these vases, like the sirens and the group composed of an old woman and a girl, here, often reappeared in *The Gates of Hell* **(11-14)**, as well as in the "black" drawings **(96-98)** executed for this decorative portal and in the engravings dating from 1881-82. Like every ornamentalist, Rodin had built up a repertory of motifs, which he used recurrently in all the artistic fields he explored.

F. B.

33

11

The Gates of Hell,
First Maquette

1880

Wax
H. 23.3 cm; W. 15.5 cm; D. 2 cm
S. 1170

In 1880, when he was still just a promising but little-known sculptor, Rodin was awarded a commission by the French state to design a bronze door for a future Museum of Decorative Arts. He threw himself body and soul into this project, drawing then modelling a multitude of subjects inspired by *The Divine Comedy*. In this long poem written in the early 14th century, Dante Alighieri (c. 1265-1321) describes his journey through Hell, Purgatory and Paradise. Like many Romantic artists before him, Rodin was passionately interested in Hell, inhabited by a multitude of despairing beings, and ignored the two others parts.

The first maquette, promptly modelled in wax, showed Rodin's initial idea for his composition. Influenced by Lorenzo Ghiberti's *Paradise* door (1425-52) for the Baptistry, Florence, he divided his portal into ten panels, five on each of the two doors, separated by ornamental friezes. No details of the contents of each panel were featured, Rodin having contented himself with sketching the general organization of his monument.

The second maquette did not show the portal in its entirety but focused on the compositional elements of some of the panels. These bas-reliefs were crowded with tiny figures. While it is impossible to identify the themes represented precisely, the relationship between several groups of figures and drawings Rodin executed during this period is obvious **(96-98)**.

F. B.

12

The Gates of Hell, Second Maquette

1880

Plastiline
H. 16.5 cm; W. 13.5 cm; D. 2.6 cm
S. 1169

13
The Gates of Hell, Third Maquette

1881

Plaster
H. 111.5 cm; W. 75 cm; D. 30 cm
S. 1189

The third maquette for *The Gates of Hell* is very similar to the composition finally retained by Rodin.
As several drawings done at this time show (96-98), the
sculptor had swiftly reduced the number of panels from
ten to eight, before abandoning the idea of compartments
on the two doors. He then borrowed some of the characteristics of Gothic art for the structure of his portal:
between the two doors there was now a central pier, sur-
mounted by a figure seated on a capital, *The Thinker* (68),
housed in a sort of tympanum. However, the work owes
its largest debt to the Renaissance, with its composition
based on orthogonal lines, its pilasters adorned with figures and its entablature supported by modillions. Among
the main groups recognizable on the doors are *The Kiss*
(33), on the left, and *Ugolino* (17) devouring his children,
on the right, in a version closer to the preliminary drawings than to the final work.

This plaster was cast from an unfired clay model, the same
one that Rodin worked on, and very probably represents
one of the last stages in the elaboration of his project.

F. B.

14
The Gates of Hell

1880–circa 1890

Bronze, cast by Alexis Rudier, 1928
H. 635 cm; W. 400 cm; D. 85 cm
Cast made for the museum collections
S. 1304

The Gates of Hell occupied
a unique place in Rodin's
œuvre. Working feverishly on this
project for several years, he created
over 200 figures and groups that
formed a breeding ground for ideas
which he drew on for the rest of his
working life. Having hoped to exhibit
his *Gates* at the 1889 Exposition
Universelle, but probably too busy to
finish them, the sculptor stopped
working on them circa 1890.

He did, however, express his desire to
complete them on several occasions.
In 1900, he decided to finally unveil
them at his first solo exhibition in
Paris. But they were shown in a fragmentary state, since he had given up
the idea of mounting the figures that
stood out the most – the individual
figures cast separately from the main
structure – because he thought they
produced too strong an effect of
contrast with the background. In
1907, *The Gates* almost saw the day
in a luxury bronze and marble version to be erected in the Musée du
Luxembourg, which housed works
purchased by the French state from
contemporary artists. Not until 1917
did Léonce Bénédite, the Musée
Rodin's first curator, manage to per-
suade the sculptor to allow him to
reconstruct his masterpiece in order
to have it cast in bronze. Rodin died
before seeing the result of all these
long years of effort.

F. B.

15

Adam

1880-1881

Bronze, cast by Susse, 1972
H. 197 cm; W. 76 cm; D. 77 cm
Cast made for the museum collections
S. 1303

In 1881, Rodin received a commission from the Ministry of Fine Arts for two large figures of *Adam* and *Eve*. He suggested placing them either side of *The Gates of Hell* **(11-14)**, possibly inspired by the arrangement of Michelangelo's *Slaves* flanking the door from the Palazzo Stanga in the Louvre. For *Adam*, he almost certainly reused an existing work, since he exhibited the statue the same year at the Salon of 1881, under the name *The Creation of Man*. Both the title and the pose of this large-scale figure attest to the enormous influence of Michelangelo's works, notably the celebrated painting of *Adam* on the ceiling of the Sistine Chapel (1508-12). The well-developed musculature, which suggests great physical strength, contrasts with the bizarre pose, which calls to mind a tormented being. Pointing his finger towards the ground, Rodin's *Adam* seems to emphasize his earthly bonds, whereas Michelangelo shows man at the moment when God confers the divine spark of life upon him.

F. B.

16

Eve

1881
Bronze, cast by Alexis Rudier, 1911
H. 172.4 cm; W. 58 cm; D. 64.5 cm
Cast commissioned by the French
state for the Musée du Luxembourg
in 1911; transferred to the Musée
Rodin in 1918.
S. 1029/Lux. 157 or 370

In his design for *The Gates of Hell* (**11-14**), dating from 1881, Rodin wanted to place *Adam* and *Eve* either side of *The Gates* as pendants. He later described how he had started to model a large female figure when he had had to stop because his sitter, who was pregnant, could no longer pose for him. He did not exhibit this unfinished statue of *Eve* until 1899, by which time he felt bold enough to show his works in a fragmentary or incomplete state. The rough surface of the skin, the lack of detail and the trace of the metal armature still visible on the right foot all attest to the fact that this was a work in progress that Rodin had decided to retain. In the meantime, he had completed a small version of *Eve*, which was exhibited in 1882 and greeted with enthusiasm. The sensuality of her body, now very smooth, in strong contrast with the modesty of the gesture she makes by lowering her head and crossing her arms, made it extremely popular. Large numbers of this statue were produced in bronze, marble and terracotta.

F. B.

17

Ugolino

a. Ugolino

Circa 1881

Plaster
H. 41.5 cm; W. 40.3 cm; D. 58.7 cm
S. 2390

b. Ugolino on a Column

1881–1900

Plaster
H. 144.5 cm; L. 40.3 cm; D. 58.7 cm
S. 2392

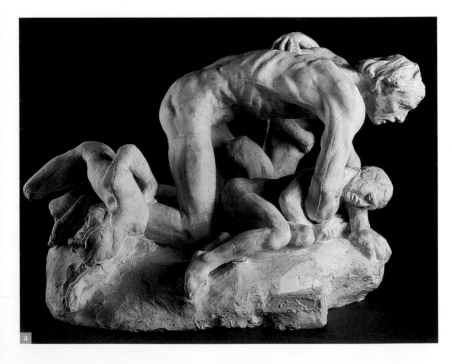

a

Rodin must have been very impressed by Carpeaux's *Ugolino* (1861, Musée d'Orsay), the famous sculpture whose dramatic subject was drawn from Dante's *Divine Comedy.* Twenty years later, after receiving the commission for *The Gates of Hell* **(11-14)**, he made several sketches of this Dantesque theme dear to the Romantics: imprisoned, driven crazy by hunger, Ugolino, Count of Gheradesca, devoured his dead children, a crime for which he was eternally damned. In his group on *The Gates* **(11-14)**, Rodin depicted the dramatic scene just before it reached its climax: Ugolino is crawling over the bodies of his dying children, but has not yet given in to his bestial instincts. Naked, grimacing, on all fours, this desperate man has lost all sense of human dignity. His pose was both humiliating and original in the art of Rodin's day. He placed this group in a prominent position on *The Gates* **(11-14)**, and then decided to have a freestanding version of it cast.

The enlargement of this group completed the process circa 1904 and the large-scale bronze now stands in the pool in the gardens of the Hôtel Biron. In 1900, for his exhibition at the Pavillon de l'Alma, Rodin showed his small-scale works on tall plaster plinths or columns, adorned with foliated scrolls. From his experiments with *The Burghers of Calais* and other sculptures, Rodin is known to have been preoccupied with both the relationship of his works to space and contrasting effects. F. B.

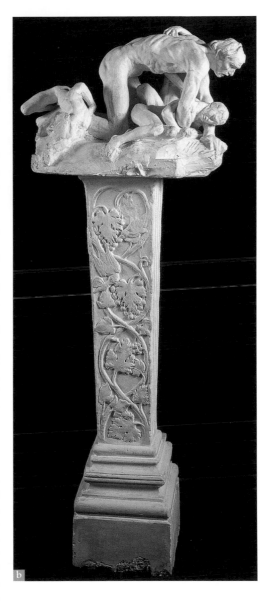

b

41

In 1883, the journalist Edmond Bazire advised Rodin to make a portrait of a famous man to help establish his own reputation. He introduced the sculptor to Victor Hugo, who refused to pose at sittings, but invited Rodin into his home on the Avenue d'Eylau and allowed him to make a few drawings of him while he was eating or having his afternoon sleep.

Rodin made sketches of the poet's head from different standpoints on the palm on his hand or on cigarette papers, before rushing out to the veranda, where he set up his sculptor's turntable in order to reproduce in clay what he had hastily jotted down. The technique of drawing from memory, which he had learnt from Lecoq de Boisbaudran, proved very useful.

The portrait was completed in 1883, two years before Hugo died. Rodin, who had always admired poets like Dante (11-14) and *Baudelaire* (41), inscribed *à l'illustre maître* on the lower neck, as if paying him a final tribute. He later reworked the bust to produce a more refined version, cut off below the frock coat's lapel, and without the base.

H. M.

18

Bust of Victor Hugo, known as the *Bust to the Illustrious Master*

1883

Bronze, cast by François Rudier, 1883
H. 48.5 cm; W. 29 cm; D. 30.5 cm
Gift of Rodin to Hugo. Acquired from Marguerite Hugo, the sitter's great-granddaughter, 1928, through David David-Weill
S. 36

One of Rodin's favourite models was Adèle Abbruzzesi, from whose supple, muscular body he drew inspiration for several strikingly sensual, female figures. Clay, which he modelled while standing in front of the sitter or which he pressed into a mould and later reworked, was the ideal material to use for a sketch, notably because of its capacity to evoke the velvety texture of the skin. With his virtuoso modelling skills, Rodin managed to convey the softness of a woman's belly, her arched back and even the weight of her breasts.

The sculptor was very fond of this study, which he completed by adding legs and arms, so as to use it as a sort of linking device on the upper left-hand corner of *The Gates of Hell* (11-14). In a slightly modified version, with a head, this torso was also used for the female figure in *Eternal Springtime* (27).

F. B.

19

Torso of Adèle

Before 1884

Terracotta
H. 11 cm; W. 37.5 cm;
D. 16.4 cm
S. 1177

20

The Burghers of Calais, First Maquette

1884

Plaster
H. 61 cm; W. 38 cm; D. 32.5 cm
S. 86

In 1347, after a year-long siege, six citizens of Calais agreed to sacrifice their lives and hand over the keys of their city to its conqueror, King Edward III of England. The story was related in Jean Froissart's *Chronicles* (1370-1400). In September 1884, the Mayor of Calais, Omer Dewavrin, suggested erecting a monument as a tribute to the heroism of Eustache de Saint Pierre and his companions, with the aid of a national appeal fund. Alphonse Prosper Isaac, a Calais-born painter who had settled in Paris, was asked to advise the monument committee on the sculptor to be chosen. He put forward Rodin's name. As soon as he started reading Froissart's account of the historic episode, Rodin began working on the project, even before the commission was confirmed. He decided not represent just *one* burgher of Calais but all *six* in a "slow procession towards death": Eustache de Saint Pierre, Jean d'Aire, Pierre and Jacques de Wissant, Andrieu d'Andres and Jean de Fiennes.

The notion of collective sacrifice was emphasized even in the first maquette. The six figures, not yet individualized, were presented on the same plane, one next to the other, with no visible order of importance and all clad in the loose garments of men about to be executed. They were placed on a very high rectangular base, adorned with bas-reliefs, which formed a triumphal pedestal. This first maquette was greeted enthusiastically by the committee. Rodin was officially awarded the commission for the monument and the price was set at 15,000 francs.

He then pursued his investigations into the identity of each figure **(21-22)** and made them express the different feelings experienced by men on the verge of death: despair, resignation, courage, impassiveness or uncertainty. He modelled them directly in their actual size, first unclothed, then clothed in the type of tunics worn by the condemned men. He arranged real shirts dipped in plaster on the nude studies, so that the bodily build could be seen under the garments.

In tandem with his figures, he worked on the heads and hands separately. These became sculptures in their own right **(23-24)**. The monument was completed in 1889, the year in which it was first presented at the Monet-Rodin exhibition in the Galerie Georges Petit, Paris **(25)**.

H. M.

21

Pierre de Wissant, Nude Study

Circa 1885

Terracotta
H. 29.6 cm; W. 16 cm; D. 16.1 cm
S. 200

This small study, modelled in lively fashion like *bozzetti*, recalls Pierre de Wissant's determined attitude. Although its arms were lost in an accident, the swaying movement of its *contrapposto* twirls the figure around on itself and shows Rodin's virtuoso modelling skills. He never made preparatory studies on paper for his sculptures, but often expressed his initial idea in sketches like these. This was the method he used for *Balzac* (50-52; 65). Several small, vigorous terracotta studies captured the poses the writer used to strike and guided the sculptor in his elaboration of the final figure.

H. M.

22

Eustache de Saint Pierre, Nude Study

Circa 1885-1886

Bronze, cast by Georges Rudier, 1964
H. 98 cm; W. 34 cm; D. 36.5 cm
Cast made for the museum collections
S. 388

Eustache de Saint-Pierre was regarded as the core fig-ure in the group of six condemned men, the oldest but also the first to risk his life by volunteering to go and hand over the keys of Calais to the victorious King of England. Here, he is represented naked, as was Rodin's usual practice before clothing his figures, half the actual size, with emaciated face and wasted body. The lively, energetic modelling accentuates the work's dramatic character, with his veins seeming to protrude from under the skin, his large knotty joints still strong. Lifting his right foot, Eustache de Saint-Pierre seems about to embark upon his heroic march.

In its energetic handling, quasi-flayed appearance, verti-cality and, to a lesser extent, its immobility, this figure seems to herald Alberto Giacometti's *Striding Man*. It has retained its autonomy and individuality, even though it was designed to be inserted in a group.

H. M.

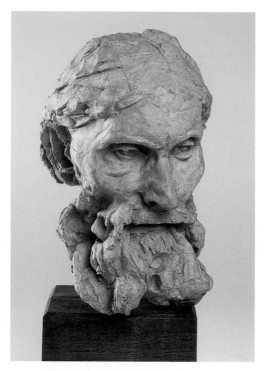

23

Eustache de Saint-Pierre,
Type A Head

1885-1886

Terracotta
H. 33.7 cm; W. 21.3 cm; D. 24.8 cm
S. 97

Rodin considered heads, like hands, to be works in their own right, the bearers of meaning and expression. He treated them with painstaking care, highlighting their independence and their force. As with his figures, he modelled them after sitters chosen according to their geographical origin. Influenced by the theory of climates expounded in the 18th century, he believed that there was a morphological type specific to each region. He therefore asked his painter friend Jean-Charles Cazin, who was born in the Pas-de-Calais region, to pose for him. His facial features and bone structure are however more easily recognizable in the second maquette than in the final version of the head.

All the energy and determination of the subject portrayed are concentrated in the sharp contours and hollow features of this head, while the medium used here, terracotta, instils an even stronger sense of presence.

H. M.

24

Pierre and Jacques de Wissant, Right Hand

Circa 1885-1886

Terracotta
H. 33.8 cm; W. 16.5 cm; D. 14.1 cm
S. 95

Rodin worked on the hands of certain *Burghers of Calais* separately so as to heighten their power of expression.

Although he used the same left and right hands for the two brothers, Pierre and Jacques de Wissant, the effect obtained on each figure was very different. Pierre de Wissant's right hand sweeps the gesture upwards, as a sign of abnegation. Jacques de Wissant's hand is drawn back towards his face, implying doubt and questioning. Isolated from the figure, the hand forms a work in its own right, not just a mere study or fragment. When Rodin decided to show it standing upright on a wooden plinth, he turned it into an independent exhibit, with a value all of its own. This is also the hand Rodin would use in *The Hand of God* (**53**), placing inside it the tiny figures of Adam and Eve who seem to emerge out of the dust.

This work became the symbol of all creation. To quote George Bernard Shaw when discussing Rodin: "*The Hand of God* is his own hand."

H. M.

25

Monument to the Burghers of Calais

1889

Plaster
H. 219.5 cm; W. 266 cm; D. 211.5 cm
S. 153

The final version of the monument was completed in 1889 and unveiled in Calais in 1895. Rodin had envisaged two possible designs for its installation: either on ground level so that the group would become "more familiar and [draw] the public into the aspect of misery and sacrifice," (Rodin, 1893), or raised on a very high plinth, so that it would stand out against the sky.

The triumphal arch of the first maquette had been eliminated (20) and the six independent figures, showing their individual feelings, were united on the same base. Confronting their destiny and death, alone, they neither touch nor look at each other. Barefoot, clad only in tunics, with a rope around their necks, the condemned men begin their slow, mournful walk.

H. M.

26

Camille Claudel with a Bonnet

Circa 1884(?)

Terracotta
H. 25.7 cm; W. 15 cm; D. 17.7 cm
S. 208

When Camille Claudel first joined Rodin's studio, she was only 20 years old. From the outset, her face captivated the sculptor, who made several portraits of the young woman, very probably that same year: *Camille Claudel with Short Hair, Camille Claudel with a Bonnet, Mask of Camille Claudel.*

The version with a bonnet was executed in various materials, from terracotta, the first stage, to bronze and glass paste, much later, in 1911. Her face, which shows "the triumphant glow of beauty and genius", a "superb" forehead, "magnificent eyes" and a "large mouth more proud than sensual" (Paul Claudel, 1951), nonetheless also reveals a sense of estrangement. By leaving traces of his working method

visible – tiny drops of clay in the corner of her eyes like tears, traces of seams from the mould, like so many scars, Rodin used the very medium of his sculpture to bring out an underlying sadness, the emotional distance the sitter had put between them, her gaze far away. As he had done with Rose Beuret and Mrs Russell, Rodin used the young woman's features in allegorical portraits such as *Aurora*, circa 1895-97 **(47)** and *France* (circa 1902-03), or in compositions that modified their meaning: *Mask of Camille Claudel with the Left Hand of Pierre de Wissant*, circa 1895 **(45)**, or *Farewell*, circa 1898 **(55)**, also known as *The Convalescent* (1906-07/1914).

A. M.

27

Eternal Springtime

Circa 1884

Bronze, cast by Alexis Rudier, 1926
H. 64.5 cm; W. 58 cm; D. 44.5 cm
Cast made for the museum collections
S. 989

Eternal Springtime was modelled during Rodin's intense period of activity for *The Gates of Hell* (11-14), but this graceful two-figure work never appeared on the portal: like *The Kiss* (33), of which it is a sort of variant, its subject evokes the happiness of two young lovers, a euphoria too inappropriate for the tragedy being played out on *The Gates*. With its rhythmic movement reminiscent of 18th-century decorative sculpture, which Rodin liked and had frequently imitated when working for ornamentalists, *Eternal Springtime* was very successful and was translated several times into bronze and marble.

The female figure of this group was based on *Torso of Adèle* (19), an earlier work modelled by Rodin and used on the tympanum of *The Gates of Hell* (11-14). Through its sensuality, this straining body with arched back fits into the composition perfectly. Responding to this ascending curve is the broad movement of the man, the dominant figure in this pair of lovers.

F. B.

28

*Young Mother
in the Grotto*

1885

Plaster
H. 36 cm; W. 28.2 cm; D. 24 cm
S. 1196

Probably modelled in 1885, the plaster was shown at the Salon the same year under the title *Woman and Love*. Several bronze and marble versions of it were made during Rodin's lifetime.

The woman and child theme was very present in Rodin's oeuvre at this time. Whether used to represent maternal love or a mythological theme, the association of the baby and the young woman was both sentimental and sensual. His chubby bodies and tender gestures, not devoid of a certain mawkishness, may be seen as a continuation of the Second Empire decorative style and a reinterpretation of 18th-century sculpture.

The roof beneath which the two figures are sheltering echoes that found in *Dried-Up Springs* (32). As a result, the two works share the same shadow effects, but their themes – the beginning and end of life – differ diametrically, this dichotomy being represented by the repetition of the figure of the old woman in *Dried-Up Springs* (32).

A. M.

29

I Am Beautiful

1882

Plaster
H. 69.8 cm; W. 33.2 cm; D. 34.5 cm
S. 1292

This two-figure group appeared in 1880 at the top of the right-hand pilaster of *The Gates of Hell* **(11-14)**. It is a combination of *Crouching Woman* **(71-72)** and *Falling Man*, whose back seems to arch under the strain of holding her in his outstretched arms. Also known as *The Abduction, Carnal Love* or *The Cat*, the group began its life as an independent sculpture circa 1882, drawing inspiration from the lines of Baudelaire's poem, "Beauty", in *Flowers of Evil*, "I am beautiful, O mortals, as a dream of stone". It illustrates Rodin's use of assemblages, which became one of the characteristic features of his working method. The sculptor thus profoundly altered the meaning of *Crouching Woman* **(71-72)**, a very open female figure whose posture may appear either obscene or erotic, by turning her over and folding her up into a closed ball, which the man lifts into the air like Atlas. The twisting movement of the male body, anatomically unrelated to the actual gesture, established parallels between the work and the studies of movement and abductions popular in 17th- and 18th-century sculpture.

A. M.

30

The Three Shades

Before 1886

Bronze, cast by Alexis Rudier, 1928
H. 97 cm; W. 91.3 cm; D. 54.3 cm
Cast made for the museum collections
S. 1191

In Dante's *Divine Comedy*, the shades, i.e. the souls of the damned, stand at the entrance to Hell, pointing to an unequivocal inscription, "Abandon hope, all ye who enter here". Rodin made several studies of *Shades*, before finally deciding to assemble three identical figures that seem to be turning around the same point. He placed them on top of *The Gates*, from where they could gaze down at the spectator, then had them enlarged to create a monumental independent group in 1904. As in *Adam* (15), whose twisting, tormented pose *The Three Shades* have borrowed, Michelangelo's influence is obvious here. The angle at which the heads fall downward is so exaggerated that the necks and shoulders form an almost horizontal line. It was through anatomical distortion like this that Rodin achieved an expressive force quite unparalleled in his time.

F. B.

31

She Who Was the Helmet Maker's Once-Beautiful Wife

1887

Bronze, cast in 1891
H. 50 cm; W. 30 cm; D. 26 cm
S. 1148/Lux. 109

Purchased by the French state in 1891, the work was transferred to the Musée du Luxembourg in 1892. Yet the first time this motif appeared was on one of the pilasters of *The Gates of Hell* **(11-14)**, in 1887. It was also found on the belly of a vase known as the *Saigon Vase* **(10)**, produced by Rodin and Desbois in 1888-89 for the Sèvres porcelain factory.

Inspired by a poem by François Villon, and presented at the Salon de la *Société Nationale des Beaux-Arts*, Paris, in 1890, the work may be linked to the aesthetic of ugliness and the *memento mori* popular in the Late Middle Ages. At a time when Rodin was still searching for his sources, this vision of human destiny, and women's fate in particular, had already been explored in this vein by Desbois. Legend has it that Rodin designed *She Who Was the Helmet Maker's Once-Beautiful Wife* as a pendant and in response to Desbois' *Misery* **(120)**. With *Clotho* **(123)**, Camille Claudel also accepted the challenge of depicting this wizened flesh, this cadaverous thinness, where what is ugly in reality becomes beautiful in the eyes of the artist, because of its expressiveness and strength of character.

A. M.

32

*Dried-Up
Springs*

Before 1889

Plaster
H. 66.5 cm; W. 55 cm;
D. 61 cm
S. 166

The work was first exhibited in 1889, at the Galerie Georges Petit, Paris, entitled "Bas-relief. Two Old Women. One of them is to be modified". The last sentence attests to Rodin's modernity: he openly declared that the work presented was unfinished and was composed of a mirror image of the same figure.

In fact, Rodin re-used the same figure as in *She Who Was the Helmet Maker's Once-Beautiful Wife* (**31**) and placed two identical figures of very elderly women opposite one another, thereby inaugurating the process of duplication that he also employed before 1886 in *The Three Shades*

(**30**). The title cruelly emphasizes their loss of fertility and brings to mind the contrasting image of young mothers and children that Rodin also explored abundantly during this period. The very shape of the draped fabric, forming the grotto in which the figures are placed, recalls the *Young Mother in the Grotto* (**28**) group, which thus constitutes a sort of pendant. Apart from the subject, in both cases the play of light and shadow features strongly and turns the work into a sort of halfway stage between very high relief and freestanding sculpture.   A. M.

*T*he *Kiss* originally represented Paolo and Francesca, two characters borrowed, once again, from Dante's *Divine Comedy*: slain by Francesca's husband who surprised them as they exchanged their first kiss, the two lovers were condemned to wander eternally through Hell. This group, designed in the early stages of the elaboration of *The Gates* (11-14), was given a prominent position on the lower left door, opposite *Ugolino* (17), until 1886, when Rodin decided that this depiction of happiness and sensuality was incongruous with the theme of his vast project.

He therefore transformed the group into an independent work and exhibited it in 1887. The fluid, smooth modelling, the very dynamic composition and the charming theme made this group an instant success. Since no anecdotal detail identified the lovers, the public called it *The Kiss*, an abstract title that expressed its universal character very well. The French state commissioned an enlarged version in marble, which Rodin took nearly ten years to deliver. Not until 1898 did he agree to exhibit what he called his "huge knick-knack" as a companion piece to his audacious *Balzac* (50-52; 65), as if *The Kiss* would make it easier for the public to accept his portrait of the writer.

F. B.

33

The Kiss

Circa 1882

Marble, commissioned by the French state in 1888, carved between 1888 and 1898
H. 181.5 cm; W. 112.5 cm; D. 117 cm
Joined the collections of the Musée du Luxembourg in 1901; transferred to the Musée Rodin in 1919
S. 1002/Lux. 132

34

Danaïd,

Circa 1885

Marble
1889-1890
H. 36 cm; W. 71 cm; D. 53 cm
Transferred to the Musée Rodin, 1918
S. 1155/Lux. 90

Modelled for *The Gates of Hell* (11-14) circa 1885, this figure was eventually excluded from the final version of the portal. Also known as *The Spring*, the sculpture was purchased by the Musée du Luxembourg, Paris, the museum reserved for works by living artists, after it was shown at the Salon in 1890. Adapting a mythological theme – the daughters of Danaos, or Danaïds, were made to fill up a bottomless barrel with water in punishment for killing their husbands on their wedding night – Rodin above all constructed a feminine landscape by highlighting the curve of the back and neck. Instead of representing the Danaïd in the act of filling the barrel, as in conventional iconography, Rodin depicts her despair as she realizes the pointlessness and absurdity of her task. Exhausted, she rests her head "like a huge sob" on her arm, while her outspread "liquid" hair, to quote Rilke, merges with the water from her overturned vase. The highly polished finish on the marble, carved by Jean Escoula, is in keeping with Rodin's love of luminous modelling, without any shadowy hollows.

A. M.

Fugit Amor is without question one of Rodin's most beautiful compositions: the two straining bodies are combined in one perfect flowing movement. This two-figure group, which appeared twice on *The Gates of Hell* (**11-14**), was exhibited as an independent work from 1887 under the names *The Dream* and *The Sphinx*, which show how closely it related to the Symbolist aesthetic of the enigmatic woman.

In the second circle of *Hell*, Dante describes the eternal wandering of couples bound by their sin of forbidden love, to which Rodin added a Baudelarian theme.

This sculptural interpretation of the fantasies and anguish of Rodin's generation was a huge success, so much so that numerous versions in bronze and marble now exist. The present marble has a particularly interesting provenance, since it was carved circa 1890 for Joanny Peytel, Rodin's banker, who was one of the patrons who gave him the most financial support.

F. B.

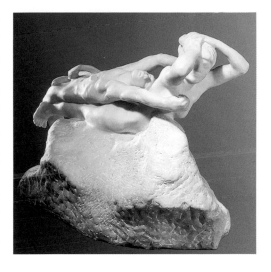

35

Fugit Amor

Before 1887

Marble, carved circa 1890
H. 51 cm; W. 72 cm; D. 38 cm
Former Joanny Peytel collection;
purchased by the museum in 1963
S. 1154

36

AUGUSTE RODIN
AND JULES DESBOIS

Ornamental Vase

Circa 1890

Bronze
H. 35.5 cm; W. 24 cm; D. 22.5 cm
Purchased by the museum, 2005
S. 6744

Rodin and Jules Desbois (1851–1935) first met in 1878 in the studio of Legrain, a young architect who was awarded several prestigious decorative commissions, and then worked together producing porcelain vases in the Sèvres porcelain factory. When Rodin set up his own studio, he employed his friend as a practitioner on a long-term basis. Circa 1890, Desbois became his main collaborator and was even entrusted with the execution of the pedestal for the *Monument to Claude Lorrain* in Nancy.

This bronze vase probably dates to the same period and is possibly an unfinished model for a decorative object. Exactly how the two artists collaborated remains unknown, but the hypothesis most frequently put forward is that Rodin designed the body of the vase, adorned with a bas-relief, and that Desbois, judging from the style of certain details, modelled the figures around the neck. However, the highly dynamic, twisting poses of the figures reveal the powerful influence Rodin exerted over his friend.

F. B.

37

Sleep

Circa 1890-1894

Terracotta, plaster, wax, nails, newspaper
H. 46 cm; W. 47.6 cm; D. 39.5 cm
S. 1829

Such composite works as this are seldom kept, since their fragility compromises their long-term conservation. Rodin, who never hesitated to employ the most varied materials, nevertheless rarely produced such a heteroclite work as this. Using a terracotta female bust as a starting point, he altered it with the help of newspaper and fresh plaster, then added wax to amend the hair and a cast of a real piece of fruit to complete his allegory. The closed eyes of this young girl, whose pose is somewhat reminiscent of *Meditation* **(48)**, as well as the pomegranate placed near her, form a perfect evocation of sleep.

The nails and the points marked in pencil show what this surprising work was originally used for: it was a model for a marble carved in 1894, which explains its uncared-for appearance. Rodin only had to indicate the broad lines of the figure to be carved to his practitioner, and the craftsman, under the supervision of the master, then had a relatively free hand.

F. B.

38

Sculptural Studies (Bozzetti)

Circa 1890-1900

a. *Right arms*, plaster,
H. 2.5 cm; W. 13 cm; D. 3.4 cm,
S. 4650 to S. 4654
b. *Right arms*, broken wrists, plaster,
H. 3 cm; W. 7.3 cm; D. 4.3 cm,
S. 4752 to S. 4757

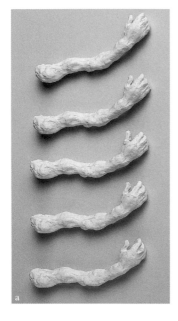

a

Rodin used the term *bozzetti* for his beloved "pieces" or sculptural studies of tiny arms, heads, legs, hands and feet, which he modelled in clay before having several casts of them made in plaster. He thus built up a repertory of forms, into which he readily delved to complete his fragmentary figures, composing new groups and assemblages in a totally unprecedented manner. This working method propels us into the heart of Rodin's creative process. Like a demiurge, the sculptor constantly composed, took apart and recreated.

There is something very modern in this approach to creating works out of pre-existing elements, made in series, so as to facilitate the artist's swift and spontaneous gesture, thus reducing the time of execution between the original idea and the creative act.

The tiny arms shown here also provide insight into the rich variety of attitudes – arms outstretched or bent at the elbow; hands clenched or open-palmed; broken wrists – and the immense creative powers of a sculptor who always started from reality to bring his works to life.

H. M.

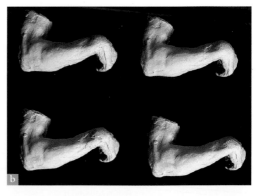

b

After Victor Hugo's death in 1885, it was decided to erect a monument in his honour in the Panthéon as a pendant to Injalbert's statue of *Mirabeau*. Rodin was awarded the commission in 1889.

The sculptor chose to depict Victor Hugo in exile, seated amongst the rocks of Guernsey, his arm outstretched as if to calm the waves. It was an image both of the poet lost in contemplation and of the champion of the Republican cause. This first project, "which lacked clarity and whose silhouette was muddled", was unanimously rejected. In 1891, the Ministry of Fine Arts found another site for it. It would eventually be erected in the gardens of Palais-Royal. From 1890 onwards, Rodin therefore worked simultaneously on two projects: the first, representing a seated Victor Hugo; the second, for the Panthéon, showing the poet standing.

It was also a nude portrait of Victor Hugo, with none of the artifice or idealization usually

39

Monument to Victor Hugo (known as the *Palais Royal Monument*)

1890

Bronze, cast by Coubertin, 1997
H. 185 cm; W. 285 cm; D. 162 cm
Cast made for the museum collections
S. 6686

seen in statues of great men. The body Rodin modelled attested to the writer's advancing years, which did not fail to shock his contemporaries.

The plaster of *Seated Victor Hugo* was shown at the Salon in Paris in 1897, alongside two of the inspirational muses, *The Tragic Muse* and *Meditation* or *The Inner Voice* (**48**), which had already accompanied the poet in the early sketches, but which were excluded from the final marble version.

H. M.

40

Monument to Victor Hugo, second project, sketch, or *The Apotheosis of Victor Hugo*

1891

Bronze, cast by Alexis Rudier, 1926
H. 116 cm; W. 52 cm; D. 63 cm
Cast made for the museum collections
S. 1066

After the rejection of his first project representing a *Seated Victor Hugo*, accompanied by muses, considered too confused by the monument committee in 1890, Rodin submitted a new project for the Panthéon: this time, the poet was clothed and standing, leaning against a pyramid-shaped rock and gazing out over the sea. Sirens from *The Gates of Hell* **(11-14)** now adorned the base, while a winged spirit in a downward-falling position hovered over the poet, like an inspirational muse. This monumental composition was better-suited to the immense space in the Panthéon transept and would have been a harmonious companion piece to Injalbert's statue of *Mirabeau*. However, the project never came to fruition, but Rodin kept the standing figure of the poet, which he reworked, unclothed, and had enlarged circa 1902.

H. M.

Rodin had a passion for model-ling from life and never worked without a sitter. When he was awarded commissions for com-memorative monuments, he there-fore used subterfuge: he looked for someone who could have been the deceased's double to employ as a model. He asked the draughtsman Louis Malteste, "who had all the characteristic features of the Baudelarian mask" (Anonymous, 1892-1), to pose for the head of Charles Baudelaire (1821-1867), originally designed for a monument – "statue, bust or medallion" (Anonymous, 1892-2), – a project which eventually fell through.

Rodin, who had illustrated *Flowers of Evil* in 1887-88, had immense respect for the poet and sought to show all of Baudelaire's genius in a simple head: "What is a statue, in fact? A body, arms and legs covered in ordinary clothes? What use are they to Baudelaire, who lived only through his mind? His head is all that matters," (Anonymous, 1892-1).

H. M.

41

Baudelaire

Circa 1892

Bronze, cast by Georges Rudier, 1969
H. 22.2 cm; W. 19 cm; D. 21.5 cm
Cast made for the museum collections
S. 32

Like so many others, the two figures of this group came from *The Gates of Hell* (**11-14**). Circa 1890, Rodin combined them to form a new independent work, which must have been an instant success, since a bronze was cast in 1891 and an enlargement, carved in marble, was commissioned in 1893 by Rodin's friend, the painter Eugène Carrière. The plaster shown here is a cast of this marble, made at Rodin's request because he liked to keep track of his works in this way – or possibly because he wanted to rework the group in other versions.

The title, *The Eternal Idol*, is very much in the Symbolist vein explored by Rodin at this time. For him, however, the form was always more important than the subject, and poetic titles like these were only given after the work was completed, sometimes in the course of discussions with writer friends.

F. B.

42

The Eternal Idol

Circa 1890–1893

Plaster
H. 73.2 cm; W. 59.2 cm; D. 41.1 cm
S. 1044

43

Christ and the Magdalen

Circa 1894

Plaster and wood model. A cloth dipped
in liquid plaster surrounds the legs
of the Magdalen. Pointed for transfer
into marble.
H. 84 5 cm; W. 74 cm; D. 44.2 cm
S. 1097

*C*hrist and the Magdalen is one of the rare surviving
sculptures inspired by religion in Rodin's oeuvre,
and possibly corresponds to a reworked version of an earlier lost *Christ*, influenced by Antoine-Augustin Préault
(1809-79).

Clinging to this emaciated, suffering Christ, whose overly
heavy head seems to have dropped sideways, is a woman,
the Magdalen, a figure originally designed for one of the
damned souls on *The Gates of Hell* (11-14), who was
then used in *Meditation* (48), the muse in *Monument to
Victor Hugo* (39-40). The present group, which would be
translated into marble for Baron Thyssen circa 1905,
underscores, as Rilke wrote, "the contrast between the
two bodies, imposed by the marble, [which] immediately
produces an impression of the boundless sadness emanating from this subject."

The Symbolistic character of the work is enhanced by it,
while the sensuality of the female figure distracts the
spectator from the subject.

H. M.

44

Iris

Circa 1895

Bronze, cast by Alexis Rudier (?),
before 1916
H. 82.7 cm; W. 69 cm; D. 63 cm
S. 1068

Designed in 1891, the figure of *Iris* was completed with a pair of wings and arranged in a swooping movement in the second project for the *Monument to Victor Hugo*, in 1897 (**40**). In 1894, however, she was enlarged, turned the right way up, placed in a vertical position and cast in bronze by Alexis Rudier, before being photographed in front of *The Gates of Hell* (**11-14**), in 1896-98.

In Greek mythology, Iris acted as a link between the world of men and the gods. Entitled *Iris, Messenger of the Gods*, or *Flying Figure*, or even *Eternal Tunnel*, the work was both Symbolistic and mythological, yet also assumed a powerful formal presence. The posi-

tion chosen by Rodin, which naturally recalls *The Origin of the World* (1866) by Gustave Courbet (1819-77), aroused not only indignation but also fascination. Weightless, energetic, the work suggests the movements of the French cancan and a gymnast stretching her limbs. The position, as well as the absence of the head and one of the arms, centre attention on the female genitalia.

A. M.

45

Assemblage: Mask of Camille Claudel and Left Hand of Pierre de Wissant

Circa 1895(?)

Plaster
H. 32.1 cm; W. 26.5 cm; D. 27.7 cm
S. 349

A woman's face was a source of inspiration for Rodin. Based on an initial portrait made of the sitter's features, the sculptor never thought twice about composing a new, symbolic work by adding another element, a helmet, for example, or a hand, as here.

The *Mask of Camille Claudel*, one of the first portraits Rodin executed of his young pupil and mistress, shows the scar-like marks left by the seam lines of the different pieces of the mould. The mask aesthetic, more than that of a head or bust, permits this focus on facial features, without the effects of hair or chest. The wide-open eyes and blank gaze however betray a feeling of distress that the addition of the colossal hand only accentuates. This hand was borrowed from *Pierre de Wissant*, one of *The Burghers of Calais* (20-25). Whereas in *The Hand of God* (53), Rodin used the right hand, here he employed the more disturbing, threatening, left hand, completely out of proportion with the face.

H. M.

46

Draped Torso
of The Age of Bronze

Circa 1895-1896

Plaster, tissue
H. 78 cm; W. 49.5 cm; D. 31 cm
S. 3179

This sculpture attests to Rodin's modernity. He played on fragmentation and readily incorporated the most diverse materials into his works – fabric, plant elements, bricks, newspaper and eggshells.

The torso shown here is a partial reworking of *The Age of Bronze* (**6**), severed at the waist and with arms removed. It is draped in the manner of Virgins, but is nevertheless a man, and the effect of the drapery around his face, which is usually employed with female models, produces a certain sense of strangeness.

The amputation of the arms, concealed by a real piece of fabric dipped in plaster, is not devoid of violence. It deprives the statue of the slightest gesture and turns it into a sort of icon.

The tear in the fabric to the side of the forehead reveals a gash, the trace of a wound incurred by this vanquished warrior.

H. M.

47

Aurora

Circa 1895–1897

Marble
H. 56 cm; W. 58 cm; D. 50 cm
S. 1019

Here we have a fine example of the way in which Rodin worked, showing how he conferred an allegorical dimension on portraits he made of people close to him, such as *Farewell*, circa 1898 **(55)**, or *France* (circa 1904), both based on the *Mask of Camille Claudel* **(45)**. The sculptor proceeded in the same manner with *Aurora*, who also borrows Camille Claudel's facial features. The face remains smooth and polished, the expression somewhat distant, while the block of marble surrounding it is deliberately left rough-hewn, with visible toolmarks. This contrast, which is reminiscent of Michelangelo's works, enabled Rodin to highlight the radiance of the face, while the title of the work evokes the sun rising at the break of day.

This composition was one of Rodin's last works inspired by Camille Claudel, executed at the time their relationship ended.   H. M.

48

Meditation
or *The Inner Voice*

1896

Patinated plaster
H. 147 cm; W. 76 cm; D. 55 cm
S. 1125

Constructed around a sinuous line, her *contrapposto* incomplete, *Meditation* originated in a figure on the tympanum of *The Gates of Hell* (11-14), inspired by Michelangelo. She was then reworked into the *Monument to Victor Hugo* (39-40), before being enlarged under the name *The Inner Voice*. She represented one of the muses who inspired the poet. In order to include her in the monument, Rodin had to remove her arms and amputate part of her legs. Outside of this context, the figure was exhibited in the same state in Dresden and Stockholm in 1897, but because of its unfinished appearance, the public found it hard to understand. Rodin, however, was extremely fond of this work, which Rilke described as follows: "The arms are surprisingly absent. Rodin felt them in this instance… to be something extraneous to the body which sought to envelop itself without any external aid… The same is true of Rodin's armless statues; nothing vital is missing. One stands before them as if before a completed whole that brooks no complement," (Rilke, 1928).

H. M.

49

Pallas with the Parthenon

1896

Marble and plaster
H. 47 cm; W. 38.7 cm; D. 31 cm
S. 1027

Rodin admired the classical beauty of Mariana Russell, the Italian wife of his friend, the Australian painter, John Russell. At his request, Rodin modelled the bust of the young woman in 1888, but he then took the initiative of re-using it as a starting point for other works. In 1889, Rodin exhibited the face alone, in the form of a silver head, and then transformed this portrait into an allegory. His sitter's regular features reminded him so much of the perfection of Antique masterpieces that he turned Mrs Russell into *Pallas with a Helmet*, an evocation of Athena, the Greek goddess of reason, knowledge and the art of war. Pursuing his investigations in this vein, he reworked a marble portrait of the young woman, placing a small plaster model of the Parthenon on her head. This was a reference to Antiquity's most famous temple, the main place of worship dedicated to the goddess in her native city of Athens. Rodin thus revived the image of the poliad divinity, the personification of a city crowned with fortifications, while proclaiming his love of ancient Greece, the unsurpassable model.

F. B.

In 1891, Rodin received the commission for a *Monument to Balzac* from the Société des Gens de Lettres, a writers' association co-founded by the author of *The Human Comedy*. The sculptor set to work with his customary enthusiasm. He began by assembling as many portraits and descriptions as he could. He then made sketches of several compositions, none of which satisfied him, and finally decided to use as a starting point the torso of a study made about ten years earlier for one of the *Burghers of Calais*, Jean d'Aire **(20-25)**. This muscular body did not correspond to the idea people had of the great writer, but Rodin was no longer looking for a physical resemblance: the tense, determined expression of this figure was what interested him, for it was meant to confer the strength of a wrestler on his *Balzac*. As usual, the sculptor worked through fragmentation and assemblage, adding legs, modifying the position of the arms, placing the hands over the genitals, trying out several heads… It was this body, draped in a dressing gown **(51)** and provided with a head **(65)**, that would enable Rodin to elaborate the final monument **(52)**.

F. B.

50

Balzac, Second Study for Nude F, known as *Nude as an Athlete*

1896

Bronze, cast by Georges Rudier, 1969
H. 93.1 cm; W. 43.5 cm; D. 35 cm
Cast made for the museum collections
S. 1080

77

51

Balzac, Study for the Dressing Gown

1897

Plaster
H. 148 cm; W. 57.5 cm; D. 42 cm
S. 146
Exhibited at the Musée Rodin, Meudon

At each stage of his creative process, Rodin studied the drapery that would cover his naked figures. Balzac was famous for the dressing gown he liked to wear at home when writing, and the Société des Gens de Lettres wished to see him depicted in it. Anxious to be accurate, Rodin used a dressing gown supplied by Balzac's tailor. He placed it on the study of his body (50), then arranged the fabric how he wanted and stiffened it, before having a cast made of it. What came out of the mould was a strange plaster ghost, an empty garment that revealed the shape of the body that it would cover. This object enabled the sculptor to model the very subtle drapery on the *Monument to Balzac* (52): what Rodin was seeking was for this part of the work to vibrate in the surrounding atmosphere, for the light to flow over its surface without creating any excessive effects of contrast. The dressing gown was thus the materialization of an aesthetic elaborated by Rodin at the turn of the century, whose flowing softness broke away from the concern for power still expressed by the head of *Balzac* (65).

F. B.

52

Monument to Balzac

1898

Bronze, cast by Alexis Rudier, 1935
H. 270 cm; W. 120.5 cm; D. 128 cm
Cast made for the museum collections
S. 1296

Having conducted his research into Balzac's body and head simultaneously, Rodin ended up with an assemblage in which these two elements conveyed their own values. While the head had evolved from a portrait resembling the writer into a concentration of expressive features **(65)**, the body had moved in the opposite direction, veering towards a dilution of form in a symphony of nuances materialized in the fluid surface of the dressing gown **(51)**.

What Rodin finally produced in 1897, after six years of labour, was a revolutionary monument. Stripped of the writer's usual attributes (armchair, pen, book…), his *Balzac* was not so much a portrait but a powerful evocation of the visionary genius whose gaze dominated the world, of the inspired creator draped in the monk's habit he used to wear when writing. This overly innovative monument caused such an outrage when it was unveiled in 1898 that the commission was cancelled. Rodin never saw his monument cast in bronze. The present cast was made in 1935 for the museum collections, while another was erected in Boulevard Raspail, Paris, in 1939.   F. B.

53

The Hand of God
or *The Creation*

Before 1898-1902
Marble
H. 94 cm; W. 82.5 cm; D. 54.9 cm
S. 988

A large right hand, itself emerging from a very rough-hewn block of marble, holds a clod of earth in which two struggling emergent figures, *Adam* and *Eve* (15-16), have been modelled. The hand of the original Creator is also that of the sculptor. Numerous features – the contrast between the highly polished areas and the rough marble, the posture of the woman reminiscent of *Dawn* in the Medici Chapel, San Lorenzo (Florence) – recall the work of Michelangelo. For the latter, a sculpture was buried in the marble and had to be extracted from it through the artist's skill, but Rodin was a modeller, which implied a different approach. *The Hand of God* seems to be a synthesis of these two very dissimilar methods. *The Hand of the Devil* forms a companion piece, while its Symbolistic title links it to a whole series of works made during the 1890s, such as *The Cathedral* (**78**) and *The Secret*.

A. M.

54

Bust of Rochefort

1884-1898

Plaster
H. 72.5 cm; W. 43.5 cm; D. 44 cm
S. 1667

The journalist Henri Rochefort (1831-1913) was a fierce opponent of the Second Empire, then a supporter of the Paris Commune, for which he was sent to a penal colony in New Caledonia. His escape, in 1874, caused quite a stir. He was granted amnesty in 1880. Rodin executed his portrait four years afterwards, when he was working on *The Gates of Hell* (11-14) and was about to begin *The Burghers of Calais* (20-25). The powerful modelling developed by the sculptor for these two monuments is also found in the *Bust of Rochefort*. Using perfectly balanced large masses, Rodin modelled only the face in detail, sketchily indicating the polemicist's garments, while handling the hair in thick locks. In 1898, he had the bust enlarged half as large again, then modified the base by placing it at a slight slant. As a result, the expression of intense concentration dominating the first portrait was considerably altered: thrust forward, the impressive forehead assumed a threatening air, while the eyes, now concealed in shadow, hardened Rochefort's gaze.

F. B.

55

Farewell

Circa 1898

Plaster
H. 38.8 cm; W. 45.2 cm; D. 30.6 cm
S. 1795

Composed of the *Camille Claudel with Short Hair* (1884) and two independent hands added in front of her face, the work attests to Rodin's fondness for assemblages, apparent in both his narrative style and his portraiture. The *Mask of Camille Claudel with the Left Hand of Pierre and Jacques de Wissant* (**45**) and the *Bust of Henry Becque* (**75**) are other examples of assemblages. This process is similar to that used in early allegorical portraits in which the spectator is unsure of what he is actually looking at.

By placing the head and hands on a block of plaster, Rodin shed light on what he thought about plinths. The present work is reminiscent of *Thought* (1886-89) and heralds 20th-century investigations by sculptors such as Giacometti.

A. M.

56

Funerary Spirit

1898(?)

Bronze, cast by Coubertin, 1981
H. 85.7 cm; W. 39 cm; D. 32 cm
Cast made for the museum collections
S. 795

Possibly complete in its original state, this fragmentary figure, which appears to be on the point of losing its balance, makes a direct reference to Antique sculpture, notably *The Spirit of Eternal Repose* (Louvre, Paris) and Skopas's figure of *Pothos* (4th century BC). The presence of a deep crack at waist level and an inconsistency behind the left leg emphasize this influence. The statue dates from the period during which Rodin produced fragmentary works, mutilating and paring down his figures to make them more forceful and expressive.

In 1899, Rodin received the commission for the *Monument to Puvis de Chavannes* **(67)**, a painter and long-standing friend whose portrait bust he had previously modelled. He included the figure of the spirit in his project, as the symbol of painting. The latter, shown in the Pavillon de l'Alma in 1900, with a left arm, was then enlarged and reunited with its head and other arm. The actual monument never saw the day.

H. M.

Extolling work and workers was an important line of thought in the 19th century, which saw the rise of the industrial and working classes. The emergence of Naturalism at the end of the century contributed to this glorification. Asked by Armand Dayot (1851-1934) and Desbois to coordinate a project for the 1900 Exposition Universelle, Rodin responded with enthusiasm. The idea of a collective project appealed to him. He understood the notion of hard work; it was a value that meant a great deal to him. As he would say in 1911, "How much happier humanity would be, if work, instead of being the ransom of existence, was its goal." This monument, designed like a staircase tower, recalls the towers of Blois, Chambord and Pisa, as well as the Trajan Column, Rome, in the way its bas-reliefs on the theme of craftsmen spiral up the shaft. The base with the crypt is also reminiscent of the Roman monument. Underground workers, miners, in particular, were to be represented on it, while mankind's other activities were depicted in an ascending movement on the column leading up to the poet, the philosopher and the artist. On the base, the figures of *Night* and *Day* symbolize work's infinite movement; on the top, *Benedictions*, later transformed into an independent group, recall that work is carried out with "love and joy". The mining accident that occurred at Courrières in 1906 revived interest in the project for a monument evoking both "hive and lighthouse", which would have been 130 metres high and had *The Gates of Hell* (11-14) for its entrance, but it never came to fruition.   A. M.

57

The Tower of Labour

1898-1899

Plaster
H. 151 cm; W. 65 cm; D. 68 cm
S. 169

58

The Martyr

Large version

1899

Bronze, cast by Alexis Rudier, 1917
H. 42 cm; W. 152 cm; D. 100.5 cm
Cast made for the museum collections
"in accordance with Mr Rodin's wishes"
S. 1160

This figure, which appeared on the lower left-hand door and on the tympanum of *The Gates of Hell* (11-14), partially draped, with eyes veiled, and representing *Fortune*, was removed from this infernal context to begin an independent existence. It was then enlarged, but still cut in the same way down the spine and on the back of the head as when it was attached to the bottom of the door.

Reclining, in an ambiguous attitude of either suffering or ecstasy, with arms apart and head falling backward, the figure is portrayed in the manner convention had demanded since Antiquity for those who died a violent death. Rodin very probably drew his inspiration here from Stefano Maderno's celebrated statue of *Saint Cecilia* (Santa Cecilia in Trastevere, Rome, 1600), but this work may also be compared to Bernini's *Lodovica Albertoni*.

The figure is neither identified, nor personalized. No detail recalls the history or death of the person portrayed. The naked body exposed to the public gaze bears no wound. The attitude of complete abandon and the facial expression with closed eyes establish parallels with Bernini's *Ecstasy of Saint Teresa*. Could Rodin's *Martyr* be the image of a woman in ecstasy, whose wounded heart is dying of love?

H. M.

Assemblages:

59

Despairing Youth and Child of Ugolino around a Vase

Circa 1900(?)

Plaster and pottery
H. 45.8 cm; W. 46.6 cm; D. 27.5 cm
S. 3614

60

Standing Female Nude in a Vase

Circa 1900(?)

Plaster and pottery
H. 47 cm; W. 20.7 cm; D. 14 cm
S. 379

These assemblages, "small floral souls that you have raised up out of antique vases", as Rilke used to say, show how creative and ingenious Rodin was, as he readily borrowed cups and vases from his collection of antiques to incorporate them into his own work.

Used in his sculpture, the pottery lost its utilitarian function. The cups and bowls were most frequently employed as receptacles for small female nude figures, placed inside them, sometimes in balanced arrangements or seated on the rim in the most varied attitudes. In the assemblage *Standing Female Nude in a Vase* (60), Rodin used the torsos of two well-known figures, *Despairing Youth* and *Child of Ugolino*, for handles.

The sculptor seems to have explored this kind of work circa 1900, giving free rein to his imagination and occasionally using these assemblages as starting points for works in marble *(Little Water Fairy, Flowers in a Vase).*

H. M.

61

Madame Fenaille

Circa 1900(?)

Plaster
H. 49 cm; W. 38 cm; D. 31.5 cm
Acquired in 2006, former
Maurice Fenaille Collection
S. 6745

62

Madame Fenaille, with Head Leaning on her Hand

1912-1913

Marble, second version,
carved by Émile Matruchot
H. 66.5 cm; W. 88 cm; D. 92.5 cm
Gift of Mme Robert de Billy, 1947
S. 1397

M aurice Fenaille, Rodin's friend and patron, was both an entrepreneur and a philanthropist, who commissioned the sculptor to model a portrait of his wife in 1898, at the time of the *Balzac* scandal, as if to show him his enduring support. This commission, following the one for the decoration of his villa in Neuilly, would result in a lengthy creative process: three terracottas and thirteen plasters gave rise to one stone and four marble versions.

Marie Fenaille was a fine-featured young woman whose portrait, executed on a small and large scale, was the starting point for several variations, occasionally differing only very slightly. The present work is not a society portrait, like those of *Mme Roll* (1887) or *Mme Vicuña* (1888), but a more personal portrait, since, in the 1890s, Rodin preferred working from faces of people close to him: Camille Claudel, Rose Beuret, Mrs Russell. Here, Rodin played on the duality of the young model, both a woman of the world and a woman friend, tilting her face to one side to emphasize her gentle, dreamy expression.

The plaster bust, recently acquired by the museum, shows how the artist constantly pursued his investigations and research, notably by reworking the hair and neck with fresh plaster because the joint seemed overly strained.

The first two marble versions are more faithful portraits of the sitter's features, whereas the two other later versions are more allegorical. It was less a question of portraying the young woman accurately than of evoking her presence. The face, hidden by the addition of a hand, seems to gradually sink further and further into the block of unhewn marble. The form seems to melt into the medium, while the handling of the work, apparently left unfinished, is an allusion to Michelangelo's sculpture.

H. M.

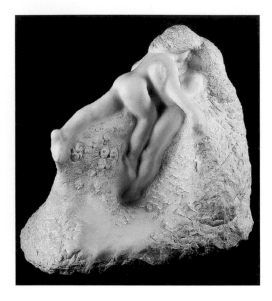

63

Nymphs Playing

Circa 1900-1910

Marble
H. 53.1 cm; W. 59 cm; D. 44.6 cm
S. 1117

The two female figures in *Nymphs Playing* came from the abundant stock of subjects modelled in the early 1880s for *The Gates of Hell* (**11-14**), but this group, composed in the early 20th century, is far removed from the infernal atmosphere inspired by Dante's *Divine Comedy*.

Employing his by-now customary working method, Rodin used two plaster figures to compose a new work, typical of his interest in unsteady poses and in the erotic quality of the assemblage of two female bodies. This work, probably simply a sketch, was, however, sufficiently erotic to serve as a model, the making of which was entrusted to one of his practitioners. These men, who were sculptors in their own right working for Rodin, carved the marble under his supervision. In *Nymphs Playing*, the practitioner demonstrated a remarkable expertise in the rendering of the various textures: the smooth skin of the female bodies contrasts with the roughness of the unhewn marble, while the transparency of the marble between the nymphs' legs responds to the polished surface of the part evoking the water of the stream at their feet.

F. B.

64

*Assemblage: Head
of Saint John the Baptist
with Three Hands
in a Medallion*

Circa 1910

Plaster and reliquary
H. 17.4 cm; W. 14 cm; D. 6.4 cm
Acquired in 1953. Gift of Mme Rudier
S. 1375

Rodin used the theme of Saint John the Baptist recurrently, as did his contemporaries. Since it was both sensual and religious, it was very successful. Rodin first handled this theme **(9)** in 1878, followed, in 1887, by the *Head of Saint John the Baptist on a Platter*.

Here, in what resembles a reliquary, Rodin has combined a reduced cast of the *Head of Saint John the Baptist* with three hands. These encircle the head like wreaths of flowers or like the paper quilling around relics in Roman Catholicism. The work is unusual; it can be linked to that slender religious thread running through Rodin's oeuvre, which was perhaps stronger than initially thought, and to his fondness for fragmentation and assemblages.

A. M.

65

RODIN AND PAUL JEANNENEY
(PSEUDONYM OF PAUL-CYPRIEN
LOEWENGUTH, 1861–1920)

*Balzac,
Monumental Head*

Circa 1897

Glazed stoneware, cast 1902-1904
H. 47 cm; W. 44 cm; D. 38 cm
S. 1934

Abandoning the idea of making a true likeness of Balzac, Rodin decided to express the writer's creative force. He focused on the main facial features (mouth, nose, arches of the eyebrows, thick masses of hair) and emphasized their relief to create a powerful effect of contrast. In so doing, *Balzac, Monumental Head* is distinguished from his body, draped in a dressing gown that the sculptor wanted to be smoothly flowing and full of nuances **(51)**.

Rodin enjoyed reworking the studies made for his major works and producing works that differed in size and medium. This is why he entrusted an enlargement of one of the final studies for the head of *Balzac* (1898) to Paul Jeanneney, a wealthy engineer turned enlightened potter, so that he could translate it into stoneware. Like his master Jean Carriès, Jeanneney had a real passion for Japanese pottery, whose texture and colour effects he succeeded in reproducing here.

F. B.

66

Head of Sorrow

Circa 1903-1904

Bronze, cast by Alexis Rudier, 1908
H. 21.7 cm; W. 22.5 cm; D. 27 cm
Cast commissioned by the French state for
the Musée du Luxembourg, Paris, in 1908;
transferred to the Musée Rodin in 1918.
S. 1127/Lux. 152

Rodin was first and foremost an exceptionally talented modeller, but in the course of his career he increasingly began to use pre-existing works in his creative process. Artists have always had recourse to dismantling and reassembling their works, but Rodin made particularly bold use of this practice, exhibiting fragments as works in their own right. Thus the head of one of the children of *Ugolino* (**17**), which also belonged to *The Prodigal Son* (**70**), was removed from its context and enlarged circa 1904 to become the *Head of Sorrow*, which seems to cry out in grief. Enlargement smoothed forms by erasing details and conferred a stronger physical presence on works.

The title of a work almost always came to Rodin after its completion and could be modified in the course of time: translated into marble, the present work was also known as *Joan of Arc*, *Orpheus* or even *Head of Medusa*.

F. B.

67

*Monument
to Puvis de Chavannes*

1899–1903

Plaster
H. 187 cm; W. 110 cm; D. 76.5 cm
S. 5417

In 1891, Rodin had modelled a bust of his friend Puvis de Chavannes, the great "decorator of walls", one of the most famous artists of his day, alongside Monet and Rodin himself. The painter died in 1898 and Rodin soon received a commission for a commemorative monument. Rodin designed an assemblage of pre-existing figures and objects: the bust of Puvis stood on two capitals, placed one on top of the other. Leaning towards the portrait bust was a large *Spirit of Eternal Repose*, also known as *Funerary Spirit* (56) picking fruit off an apple tree, which symbolized both the painter's renown and the well-deserved peace he had just been granted. Reference to the Antique, so dear to Puvis, dominated this bold installation: the superposition of architectural elements alludes to the stacks of pieces found on archaeological sites, while the *Spirit* derived from an ancient statue in the Louvre.

Rodin never finished this monument, but it may have served as a source of inspiration for Alberto Giacometti's astonishing *Surrealist Table* (1933).

F. B.

68

The Thinker

1903

Bronze, cast by Alexis Rudier,
1904
H. 180 cm; W. 98 cm; D. 145 cm
Transferred to the Musée Rodin
in 1922
S. 1295

When conceived in 1880 in its original size (approx. 70 cm) as the crowning element of *The Gates of Hell* (11-14), seated on the tympanum, *The Thinker* was entitled *The Poet*. He represented Dante, author of the *Divine Comedy* which had inspired *The Gates*, leaning forward to observe the circles of Hell, while meditating on his work. *The Thinker* was therefore initially both a being with a tortured body, almost a damned soul, and a free-thinking man, determined to transcend his suffering through poetry. The pose of this figure owes much to Carpeaux's *Ugolino* (1861) and to the seated portrait of Lorenzo de' Medici carved by Michelangelo (1526-31).

While remaining in place on the monumental *Gates of Hell*, *The Thinker* was exhibited individually in 1888 and thus became an independent work. Enlarged in 1904, its colossal version proved even more popular: this image of a man lost in thought, but whose powerful body suggests a great capacity for action, has became one of the most celebrated sculptures ever known. Numerous casts exist worldwide, including the one now in the gardens of the Musée Rodin, a gift to the City of Paris installed outside the Panthéon in 1906, and another in the gardens of Rodin's house in Meudon, on the tomb of the sculptor and his wife.

F. B.

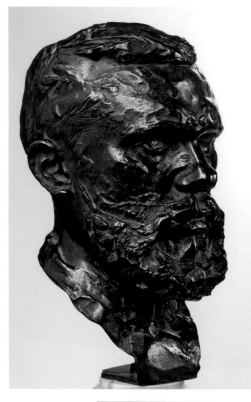

69

Gustave Geffroy

1905

Bronze, cast by Alexis Rudier, 1905-1907
H. 34 cm; W. 17 cm; D. 22 cm
S. 34

Gustave Geffroy (1855–1926) was a man of letters, journalist and art critic. He wrote a biography of Monet, promoted the works of Cézanne and met Rodin in 1883, shortly after having written a highly complimentary article on the sculptor. This was the beginning of a long friendship, during which Geffroy showed how well he understood and analysed not only Rodin's work but also, if necessary, Camille Claudel's. Geffroy's portrait seems to have been done to thank the critic for his loyal support in *The Thinker* (**68**) affair, when a committee was formed to erect the sculpture outside the Panthéon. The firm, decisive modelling on the view of the head, with a sketchily indicated neck, highlights the critic's intelligence and concentration. The bronze still bears traces of the pellets of clay that add relief to the surface but also demonstrate how important the medium was in Rodin's creative process.

A. M.

70

The Prodigal Son

Circa 1886

Large model (1905)
Bronze, cast by Alexis Rudier, 1942
H. 138 cm; W. 87 cm; D. 75 cm
Cast made for the museum collections
S. 1130

Taut as a bow string, this male figure originated in the *Ugolino* group **(17)**, designed for the *The Gates of Hell* **(11-14)**. Placed upright for the man in *Fugit Amor* **(35)**, the head and torso belong to one of the children of *Ugolino*, reworked with different legs. The head was again re-used in *Head of Sorrow* **(66)**. This method of composing new works out of pre-existing fragments was central to Rodin's creative process.

The enlargement of the work is even more dramatic and its form is perfectly in keeping with the subject borrowed from the New Testament parable of the spendthrift son who returns home to throw himself at his father's feet and beg his forgiveness for the ingratitude with which he had previously treated him. By highlighting certain details of this figure, like the hands, and by placing it in an unbalanced position, Rodin infuses this sorrowful body with the irrepressible fervour of a final prayer.

F. B.

71

Crouching Woman,
also known as *Lust*

Circa 1881–1882

Terracotta
H. 25.5 cm; W. 21 cm; D. 21 cm
S. 109

72

Crouching Woman
Large model
1906–1908

Bronze, cast by Alexis Rudier, 1909
H. 85.8 cm; W. 60 cm; D. 52 cm
Transferred to the Musée Rodin
by the French state, 1918
S. 1156/Lux. 367

Crouching Woman, purchased by the French state at the Salon of 1909 for the Musée du Luxembourg, bears witness to Rodin's working method. The original figure, conceived for the tympanum of *The Gates of Hell* (11-14), looks like a compact block with limbs gathered together and pressed tightly against the torso. This block-like sculpture reflects Rodin's aesthetic analysis of Michelangelo's sculpture: it is a work that, to quote the great Italian artist, could roll down a hill without breaking. One of the earliest figures modelled for *The Gates of Hell* (11-14), it was enlarged and slightly modified several years after its conception.

In its simultaneously open and closed posture, the figure is representative of the raw eroticism expressed in some of Rodin's works during this period. Not the eroticism found in his figures of naiads or *The Kiss* (**33**), but a dark, disturbing sexuality, often regarded as obscene because of the muffled violence that seems to emanate from the sculpture.

The quasi-animal sensuality of this figure, nicknamed the "frog", or a "batrachian" by some of Rodin's contemporaries, is what made it so successful. Rodin reworked it in different materials and sizes, for example in *I Am Beautiful* (**29**) and *The Fallen Caryatid carrying her Stone* or *The Fallen Caryatid with Urn*.

A. M.

73

The Walking Man

1907

Bronze, cast by Alexis Rudier, 1913
H. 213.5 cm; W. 71.7 cm; D. 156.5 cm
S. 998

This work with a complex genesis illustrates how receptive Rodin was to the English sculptor Henry Moore's belief that an artist should "reconsider and rethink" an idea. Also known as *Saint John the Baptist* or *First Impression*, the sculpture was conceived in 1899-1900, using studies for the torso and legs of *Saint John the Baptist* (9), dating from 1878. The original clay torso, modelled around about this time, too, was apparently rediscovered circa 1887; the legs also belonged to the early studies of *Saint John*. Despite the differences in the condition of these elements, Rodin assembled them in the late 1890s.

The resultant figure is marginally out of true; the torso leans forward and swivels slightly to the left. The impression of movement is heightened by the barely perceptible inaccuracy of the adjustments. The missing arms reinforce the effects sought by the artist who broke away from the hallowed academic tradition of "full figure" sculptures. The choice of a more universal title shows Rodin's concern for expressing something essential rather than fortuitous or specific, as in *Saint John the Baptist*.

A. M.

Taking part in public competitions was the best way for a young sculptor to earn a reputation and commissions. In 1879, Rodin submitted two projects, *Bellona* (8) and *The Call to Arms*, also called *The Defence*, to the competitions launched by the French state for a *Monument to the Republic* and a *Monument to the Defence of Paris*.

A design for an "allegorical monument representing the Defence of Paris in 1870", to be erected at the Rond-point de Courbevoie, *The Call to Arms* is a depiction of a naked, wounded soldier, who vividly recalls the figure of *Christ* in Michelangelo's *Pietà* (now in the Museo dell'Opera del Duomo, Florence). He is supported by a winged genius, whose furious expression, horizontal outstretched arms and clenched fists recall Rude's *Genius of Liberty*, on the Arc de Triomphe. Rodin's group was eliminated in the first round, the jury preferring the more conventional, more balanced entry from Louis-Ernest Barrias. It "must have seemed too violent, too strident. So little road had been covered since Rude's *Genius of Liberty* that also shrieks with all her strength," Rodin admitted in 1917.

The group was enlarged to double its size in 1912, before being reworked and further enlarged between 1917 and 1919, for a Dutch monument committee, who then donated it to the city of Verdun.

H. M.

74

The Call to Arms

1912-1918

Bronze, cast by Alexis Rudier, 1917
H. 230 cm; W. 116 cm; D. 84.5 cm
Cast for the museum collections
"in accordance with Mr Rodin's wishes";
gilded in 1937 to be placed at the far end
of the gardens, on the south side
S. 1301

75

Bust of Henry Becque

Circa 1907

Plaster
H. 69.2 cm; W. 46.5 cm; D. 47 cm
S. 1827

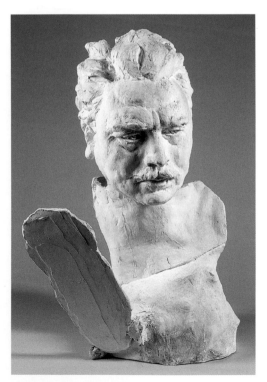

Rodin, who had made a portrait bust of Henry Becque in 1883, decided to use it again when he received a commission for a monument to commemorate the playwright, in 1904. At the time, the sculptor was passionately interested in the effect of monumentality obtained through the enlargement of a work, which accentuated the play of volumes by eliminating the details. In the case of Becque's bust, the already highly structured forms of the face and hair assumed a surprisingly geometric appearance. Rodin went one step further by cutting off the head and assembling it with the highly distinctive neck of *The Shade* **(30)** that he placed upright. The face, balancing on the edges of this neck that does not belong to it, seems to hover like a strange apparition. For some unknown reason, Rodin then added a sort of plaster palette to the base which only reinforces this fascinating work's air of mystery. Exactly where this bust fits into the elaboration process of the *Monument to Henry Becque* also remains unknown.

F. B.

76

Bust of Hanako, Type F
1907-1911
Plaster
H. 47.8 cm; W. 24 cm; D. 31 cm
S. 578

Rodin met the Japanese dancer and actress, Hanako, during the Colonial Exhibition in Marseilles, in 1906. Fascinated by the force of her expression in the scenes where she performed hara-kiri, the sculptor begged her to pose for him. In tandem with the series of studies of the actress' face as she committed suicide on stage, he also modelled this splendid portrait bust. The sketchily indicated shoulders and the very sober base, a simple mass of clay sliced with a wire, highlight the head, mounted on a strong neck. As a collector of Japanese art, Rodin enjoyed scrutinizing the features of this tiny, energetic woman and retranscribing them in broad volumes before adding the details by making fine incisions in the clay. Her hairstyle clearly interested him for particular care was paid to the top-knot. In the series of nude studies Rodin made of Hanako, this hairstyle is one of the performer's distinctive features.

F. B.

77

Pensive Bust of the Duchesse de Choiseul

1908

Terracotta
H. 39.4 cm; W. 36 cm; D. 22.2 cm
S. 1041

Rodin showed his sense of humour at the exhibition in Grosvenor House, London, by placing back-to-back the two versions, pensive and smiling, of his bust of the *Duchesse de Choiseul.*

The American-born Claire Coudert (1864-1919) married Charles-Auguste de Choiseul-Beaupré in 1891, in New York, before becoming a duchess in 1909. She burst into Rodin's life shortly before 1907 with a vitality that swept the old master off his feet. Until 1912, she exerted a very powerful influence over the sculptor and gradually cut him off from his friends and relations. She took Rodin's business dealings in hand, even making declarations such as, "Rodin! I am Rodin!" (Tirel, 1923). The sculptor began working on her bust in 1908. After the first pensive, slightly austere version, shown here, he soon moved on towards a smiling, cheerful portrait of the sitter, no doubt more in keeping with reality. With prominent cheekbones, raised eyebrows and open mouth, it is as if the sitter had been caught laughing, possibly laughing at herself. This jovial side of Claire de Choiseul's personality is heightened in the marble carved in 1911: the reference points transferred onto the stone, placed on the tips of the breasts, were retained by Rodin.

H. M.

78

The Cathedral

1908

Stone
H. 64 cm; W. 29.5 cm; D. 31.8 cm
S. 1001

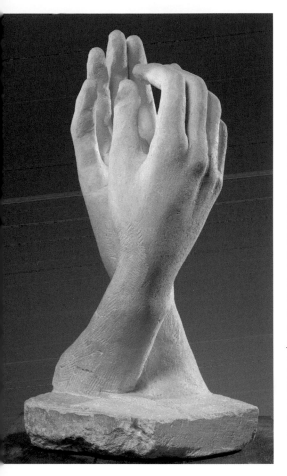

Carved in stone and still covered in toolmarks, *The Cathedral* is a combination of two right hands, belonging to two different figures. It was entitled *The Ark of the Covenant*, before being named *The Cathedral*, very probably after the publication of Rodin's *Les Cathédrales de France*, in 1914. Parallels may be drawn between the mysterious inner space that seems to emanate from the composition and Gothic architecture. Emptiness was a factor that Rodin used to allow for, and, as Rilke pointed out, "the role of air had always been extremely important" for him (Rilke, 1928).

Very similar to *The Secret*, this work belongs to the series carved in marble, most frequently after 1900, such as *The Hand of God* **(53)**, *The Hand of the Devil*, *Hands of Lovers* and *Hand from the Tomb*. But, more broadly, it emphasizes Rodin's fondness and passion for these hands, which he isolated, like the fragments in his collection of Antiques, in order to give them a more finished and autonomous form.

H. M.

During the Whistler exhibition inaugural dinner held in London, in 1905, it was decided to erect a monument to the painter James McNeill Whistler (1834-1903). The commission went to Rodin, who, in 1903, had been unanimously elected president of the International Society of Painters, Sculptors and Gravers, the association founded by Whistler in 1897.

Rodin decided to pay tribute to the painter's genius, not through a conventional portrait, an effigy or historical scene, but through an allegorical figure, a "Muse climbing the mountain of fame", the model for which was Gwen John, a young Welsh painter.

This design, which paved the way for a whole new concept of the public monument, resulted in a large-scale, armless, nude figure, exhibited at the Salon, where it was criticized for its unfinished appearance. The sculpture should have been reworked, but on Rodin's death, the monument was still not complete.

H. M.

79

Monument to James McNeill Whistler

Study for the *Naked Muse*, without Arms

1908

Bronze, cast by Coubertin, 1986
H. 223.5 cm; W. 90 cm; D. 109.5 cm
Cast made for the museum collections
S. 3005

80

Torso of a Young Woman with Arched Back

Large model

1909

Bronze, cast by Alexis Rudier, 1910
H. 86 cm; W. 48.1 cm; D. 32.2 cm
State purchase, 1910;
Musée du Luxembourg, 1911;
transferred to the Musée Rodin, 1919
S. 1064/Lux. 263

This torso comes from a full-length figure known as *Thunderstruck Damned Woman.*

The subsequent enlargement further highlights the curve of the arched back and the bust. The fin-like protuberances visible on the hips are what remains of the hands on the original small figure. Rodin decided to retain them as traces of a previous state and his working method. These processes of fragmentation and enlargement, other aspects of the artist's modernity, show how well Rodin exploited all the potential of a piece of sculpture and modified our perception of it.

Such an approach was part of the investigations, carried out by the artist in 1890-95, into fragmenting and reducing forms to the essential. For Rodin, it was not a question of leaving a work unfinished, or of leaving a figure incomplete, but of eliminating everything that was not strictly necessary in order to make its expressiveness more forceful. This no doubt explains why the torso would be so influential in the 20th century.

This cast, made during Rodin's lifetime, has a surprising grainy, matt green patina, which endows this fragmentary work with a character similar to that of findings from an archaeological dig.

H. M.

81

Fish Woman and Torso of Iris on Foliated Plinth

Circa 1908-1909(?)

Plaster, with pink patina on the plinth
H. 164.1 cm (group, 46.1 cm); W. 32.7 cm;
D. 38 cm
S. 2701

Always concerned with how his works were presented, Rodin reflected at length on the relationship between the sculpture and the base. The exhibition of his works at the Pavillon de l'Alma, Paris, in 1900, provides a magnificent demonstration of this: he showed several plasters on foliated plinths, quadrangular pillars or columns adorned with hearts, which he re-used at the exhibitions in Prague in 1902 and Düsseldorf in 1904.

He pursued his investigations even further, seeking to combine the sculpture and its base in a single composition, the base thus becoming an integral part of the work.

In the two-figure assemblage, *Fish Woman and Torso of Iris*, the group is in white plaster and the plinth has a pink patina. This contrast creates an aesthetic colour effect that only contributes to the sculpture's charm.

H. M.

82

Fish Woman

1917

Marble carved by Victor Peter
H. 34 cm; W. 34.1 cm; D. 43.5 cm
S. 1103

*F*ish Woman was made out of the enlarged head of a small female torso. Placed on a brick that acted as a base, it served as a model for the marble, which is much smoother and more decorative in appearance.

The treatment of the base, minimally rough-hewn and leaving visible toolmarks, produces an effect of contrast with the far more polished, delicately handled, upper part of the sculpture. The present marble is a replica of the original, sold by Rodin in 1915 to Mrs Spreckels through the American dancer and choreographer, Loie Fuller (now in the California Palace of the Legion of Honor, San Francisco).

Some consider this "decorative fantasy" to be an unfinished project for a fountain, an idea suggested by the way in which the subject is represented, with open mouth and wave-like hair around the face. Others see it as a study in connection with *The Gates of Hell* (**11-14**), since the theme of heads emerging out of water is frequently found in Dante's poem.

H. M.

83

Helene von Nostitz

1911

Glass paste
H. 23.2 cm; W. 21.5 cm; D. 9.7 cm
S. 991

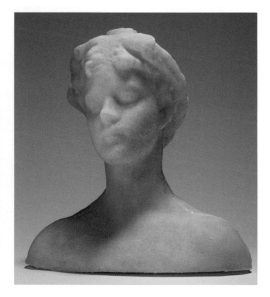

Helene von Nostitz, born Hindenburg (1878–1944), granddaughter of the German ambassador to Paris, met Rodin in 1900 at the Exposition Universelle. A very cultured young woman, knowledgeable about literature and music, she introduced the sculptor to her favourite writings. Thus began a very intellectual friendship. The first bust of the countess was modelled in 1902. When she returned to Paris, in 1907, she posed for him again, this time for longer sittings. After the marble, carved in 1908, Rodin went back to the original bust and had a glass paste version of it made by Jean Cros, son of Henri Cros, who had developed this technique. Other busts or heads – *Hanako* (**76**), *Rose Beuret* and *Camille Claudel* – were also translated into this experimental medium. The introduction of both translucidity and colour modified the work. These investigations were important to Rodin. Like many artists of his day, he explored the possibilities offered by other media, such as stoneware, which enabled him to experiment with colour and textural effects and bring sculpture closer to decorative art.

A. M.

84

Mozart, also known as *Eighteenth-Century Man*

1911

Marble
Signed and dated *A. Rodin*
H. 50.9 cm; W. 99.7 cm; D. 58 cm
S. 1085

The portrait was inspired by the head of the composer Gustav Mahler, whose bronze bust Rodin had made in 1909. Shown at the Salon that same year entitled *Eighteenth-Century Man,* by 1914 it was known as the marble bust of *Mozart.* Like many of the works dating from this period, the portrait of *Puvis de Chavannes,* for example, the head emerges from a block of very rough-hewn marble and the sculptor plays on the contrasting surfaces of the stone.

However, the manner in which the present portrait was conceived is perhaps worth emphasizing. The face of Gustav Malher became that of Music itself, incarnated by Mozart, the absolute musician. The portrait thus turns into a sort of allegory, which is by no means rare in Rodin's work; one may recall *France* and *Aurora* **(47)**, with the face of Camille Claudel, or the portraits using Mrs Russell as a starting point.

A. M.

Georges Clemenceau (1841–1929), the left-wing politician appointed prime minister in 1906, was acquainted with contemporary artists such as the Nabis, Renoir and Monet. Manet, Vallotton and Troubetzkoy sought to capture his image, but the model himself considered the painter Eugène Carrière's portraits of him to be "the least unsatisfactory".

Commissioned from Rodin by the Argentinian government, who wished to thank Clemenceau for the series of lectures he had given in South America in 1909, the portrait bust gave rise to several studies and variants: "In the room he used as a studio, ten or so clay heads of Clemenceau, cut off at the neck, stood on turntables and consoles. It was incredible... Rodin sculpted as an engraver produces aquatints, in states. In order not to 'tire' his clay with numerous amendments, he had several casts made, experimented on these successive copies and thus reworked them ten or even twelve times..." (Cladel, 1936).

Clemenceau did not like his bust. He said that Rodin had made him look like a soldier of Napoleon's old guard and refused to let him show it at the Salon of 1914.

H. M.

85

Georges Clemenceau

1911–1913

Terracotta
H. 29.6 cm; W. 27.2 cm; D. 22 cm
S. 2120

86

Dance Movement B

Circa 1911

Plaster
H. 34 cm; W. 11 cm; D. 12.5 cm
S. 1184

Sculpture and dance draw on the same religious sources, which explains the occasionally unexpected closeness of the two art forms. The series of nine *Dance Movements, A to I*, belongs to the final area of research in Rodin's life. Fascinated by the female body and movement, the sculptor took a keen interest in ballet whenever it was not classical. He first saw Alda Moreno, the woman acrobat and dancer employed at the Opéra-Comique, Paris, in 1905, in photographs, but only managed to actually meet her with the help of Jules Desbois in 1910. Over a three-year period, he made sketches and models of her, but this work, which he considered highly innovative and entitled *The Creation of Woman*, was for his eyes only. For a long time, therefore, the general public were unaware of the series, in which human anatomy is not respected so as to attain, to quote Rodin, "almost pure mathematics".

A. M.

87

Nijinsky

1912

Plaster
H. 17.5 cm; W. 9.39 cm; D. 6.5 cm
S. 1185

The second public performance of Debussy's *L'Après-midi d'un faune* in 1912 was enthusiastically applauded by Rodin. He was particularly impressed by the dancer and choreographer Vaslav Nijinsky (1889–1950), just as he had previously been fascinated by Loie Fuller, Isadora Duncan and the Cambodian dancers. The ground-breaking work of these different dancers and the exoticism of the Far-Eastern ballets provided him with a new repertory of gestures and movements which he studied through drawings and sculptures.

Nijinsky supposedly agreed to pose for him, probably in July 1912, to thank the sculptor for the support he had given him during the controversy over the Ballets Russes then raging in the press. The dancer is depicted here gathering momentum, drawing all his weight together in his heart, ready to leap into the air. The spectator is thus confronted by a person, who, in Rilke's words, "pressing down on this center, would lift himself up and share himself out into movements, no, who would immediately take them all back." It should be noted, however, that this interpretation was called into question in the 1980s, because the dance movement portrayed in the sculpture was not part of Nijinsky's repertoire. A. M.

88

Lady Sackville-West

1913

Marble, 1915
H. 57 cm; W. 75 cm; D. 57 cm
S. 809

Lady Sackville-West (1862-1936) was a loyal friend of Rodin's from 1905 onwards. She was one of those wealthy, elegant society women in Rodin's entourage who formed the basis of his clientele for portraits, after 1900. The sculptor met her again in London in May 1913, and the bust, commenced the following autumn, required numerous sittings. These resulted in several versions in clay, plaster and marble, in which Rodin varied the facial expressions and positions, as he had also done with the portrait of Mme Fenaille. Lady Sackville-West was not at all pleased with the face that Rodin modelled, claiming that she did not recognize herself and looked like a "fat negress".

In the first marble version, carved by Rodin's practitioner Rousaud, the scarf wound generously around her neck acts as an altar of repose. The facial expression hovers between a dreamlike state and sleep. Her face and pose with head tilted to one side recall the earlier work, *Sleep*.

A. M.

89

Étienne Clémentel

1916

Bronze, cast by Alexis Rudier, 1916-1917,
known as the *first state*
H. 55.4 cm; W. 54.8 cm; D. 30.2 cm
Gift of Étienne Clémentel, 1918
S. 1366

Deputy for Puy-de-Dôme from 1900 to 1919, senator from 1920 until his death, in turn Minister of Agriculture, Finance, Trade and Industry, Mayor of Riom, and Clemenceau's great friend, Étienne Clémentel (1864-1936) was very close to Rodin, to whom he was introduced by Henri Charles Étienne Dujardin-Beaumetz in 1905-06. Named by the sculptor as one of the three executors of his will, he played a dynamic role in the foundation of the museum.

This was the last portrait bust executed by Rodin before the stroke he suffered in July 1916 left him physically and mentally weakened. The unfinished bust could have been completed by Jules Desbois, but was eventually left in the present state, since the latter refused to touch Rodin's work. The different versions of Clémentel's bust indicate the sculptor's working method: the portraitist who built up a solid overall structure, before working on the various details – moustache, eyebrows, or other features – to bring out the sitter's personality and sometimes modify, almost imperceptibly, the insight one may have into the person represented.

A. M.

The Birth of Venus.
Circa 1900
Pencil, ink and watercolour
on paper
D. 4093

François BLANCHETIÈRE, Nadine LEHNI

Drawings, Paintings, Engravings

Rodin was a prolific draughtsman, producing some 10,000 drawings, over 7,000 of which are now in the Musée Rodin, Paris. His drawings were seldom used as studies or projects for a sculpture or monument. The draughtsman's oeuvre developed in tandem with the sculptor's.

Although the works on paper can only be shown periodically, owing to their fragility, the role they played in Rodin's art was by no means minor. As the sculptor himself said at the end of his life, "It's very simple. My drawings are the key to my work," (Benjamin, 1910).

Rodin never dated his drawings and only exhibited them on rare occasions from 1899 onwards, which makes any attempt to draw up a precise chronology very problematic. However, it is possible to determine the major stages in the development of his graphic oeuvre. After his years of training (1855-65), his youthful works (1870-80) included studies after Michelangelo, decorative designs for ceramics for the Sèvres porcelain factory and architectural drawings.

The important series of "black drawings" in the early 1880s were based on his initial studies for *The Gates of Hell* **(11-14)**.

From the early 1890s onwards, Rodin stopped producing drawings from his imagination and began executing simplified life drawings, gradually invaded by coloured ink washes, dominated by yellow and pink.

The majority of the drawings in the museum collection date from the extremely fertile late period (1896-1917). For the most part, they resulted from his desire to capture truth, life itself, on paper, as near, as close as possible to his models: in the space of a few minutes, he thus skilfully jotted down spontaneous drawings, without even looking at his sheet of paper. He then transferred all the vital energy he had captured in these initial drawings into a masterfully controlled, fine pencil line drawing, most frequently highlighted with watercolour. This constant dialectics between capturing the human form in movement and emphasizing a plastic vocabulary is what gives Rodin the draughtsman such a firm foothold in modernity.

N. L.

90

Dirt Track to Watermael through the Forest of Soignes

1871-1877

Oil on paper mounted on cardboard
H. 36.5 cm; W. 27 cm
P. 7240

After the siege of Paris in 1870, Rodin went to live in Brussels for six years, working, alongside Carrier-Belleuse, on decorative sculpture. This was a time when he was still attracted to painting and, being very fond of the Brabant countryside, he executed about 30 landscape views, a little-known aspect of the great sculptor's oeuvre. Rodin later told Bourdelle "[I visited the museums and cities of Belgium, but all I brought back was] a love of nature as a result of long walks and the severity of the woods that pleased me," (Cladel, 1936). These paintings were executed in the open air during the hours he spent rambling in the forest of Soignes with Rose Beuret. In this study, a path lined with a few trees, a vague silhouette of a person in the foreground, a distant grove, a parish church standing on the horizon beneath a misty sky are all depicted very freely with bold touches of bright colour. What the artist above all sought to convey was an impression of fleetingness and spontaneity.

N. L.

91

*Golden Twilight on the Dunes
in the Forest of Soignes*

1871–1877
Oil on paper mounted on cardboard
H. 27 cm; W. 34 cm
P. 7225

In this landscape, which may recall Gustave Moreau's quasi-abstract sketches or the visionary quality of Turner's atmospheric works, Rodin's handling is so free that the motif seems to dissolve into the vague patches of warm colour. When discussing this type of work, the journalist Sander Pierron spoke of "cosmic impressions" or "the symphonic richness of polychromy, combined with a poetry that characterizes a clearing in autumn," (Pierron, 1935).

Rodin's experiments with painting did not last very long, as Rilke pointed out: "In the beginning [Rodin] set up his easel anywhere, and painted. He soon realized that in so doing everything escaped his attention: life, scope, metamorphoses, the trees growing larger, the mist coming down, all the harmonious variety of events; he realized that when painting, he was exposed to the world like a hunter confronted by his prey, whereas when observing the world, he was part of it…" (Rilke, 1905).

N. L.

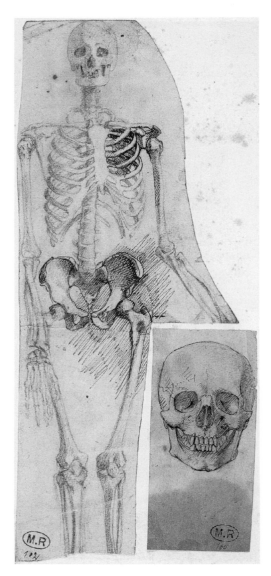

92

Skeleton and Skull

Circa 1856

Black pencil, pen and black ink on paper,
cut out and pasted on a support
H. 25.3 cm; W. 11 cm
D. 100, D.102

A very early passion for drawing, when he was barely nine, is what seems to have distinguished and set the young Auguste apart from his modest, hard-working family. "As far back as I can remember, when I was young, I used to draw. A grocer from whom my mother used to buy wrapped his prunes in paper bags made out of the pages of illustrated books, even ones with engravings. I used to copy them. They were my first models," (Dujardin-Beaumetz, 1913).

As soon as Rodin could concentrate on learning how to draw, in 1854, when he began attending the " Petite École", he was taught how to draw from memory and also encouraged to practise copying engravings and drawings.

Skeleton and Skull is composed of two copies he made during his years as a student, sketches the young artist cut out and assembled together at a later date. The very precise ink line drawing and use of fine, regular hatchings were ways of reproducing the techniques involved in engraving, while Rodin's fascination for the skeleton conveyed his desire to discover the underlying structures of the human body, beneath the visible outer layer of flesh.

N. L.

93

Sheet of Studies

Circa 1875–1876(?)

Pencil, pen and brown ink, brown wash
and gouache, on five pieces of paper,
cut out and mounted on a page
in an album later taken apart
H. 26.4 cm; W. 33.3 cm
D 274 to D 279, on the verso

Rodin's journey to Italy in 1876-76 was a decisive moment in his career. In a letter he sent to his companion, Rose Beuret, he wrote, "To tell you that since my first hour in Florence I have been making a study of Michelangelo will not surprise you, and I believe that the great magician is giving up a few of his secrets to me." Rodin filled many "pocket-sized" sketchbooks with a huge variety of tiny drawings, which he later cut out and rearranged in a different order – the logic of their juxtaposition is sometimes obscure – and then pasted onto the sheet of an album.

In the semi-reclining figure on a pediment, at the top of the sheet, and in the figure lying on a support, further to the right, it is easy to recognize the twisting movements and contorted poses inspired by Michelangelo, expressing the torments of the human condition, translated by Rodin in a network of fine entangled lines, penned quickly in ink. The *Virgin and Child*, on the left, seems to have borrowed the posture of Michelangelo's *Moses*. To bring these figures to life, the search for that condensed passion, which Rodin talked about in his conversations with Paul Gsell, is combined with the skilful modelling, subtly rendered by contrasting colour effects. These figures – which are not projects for works in another medium – show how freely Rodin drew his inspiration from the Italian master's models, but without ever copying them.

N. L.

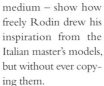

94
Vase adorned with Putti
Circa 1879-1882
Charcoal on paper
H. 38.4 cm; W. 33.1 cm
D. 7676

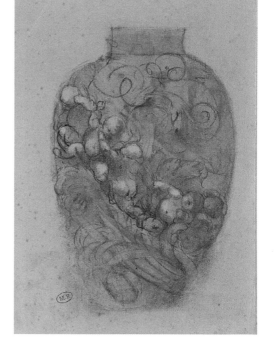

Rodin worked on several occasions in decorative sculpture studios, where his skills as a draughtsman and modeller were highly appreciated. This decorative design for a vase dates from 1879-82, when Rodin was employed at the Sèvres porcelain factory by Albert Carrier-Belleuse. It may be related to the *Vase of the Elements*, whose form was invented by Carrier-Belleuse in 1880, but whose decoration was designed and executed by Rodin. In both works, the decoration mixes traditional *putti* – chubby cherubs at play – with foliated volutes whose dynamic lines structure the composition.

The technique employed in this drawing resembles that of the "black drawings", which Rodin produced in profusion during this period: through his use of strong contrast, the bright highlights of the reliefs (belly, buttocks, arms and legs of the *putti*) stand out against the dark background of the vase. A similar effect is found in the "paste-on-paste" relief designs made by Rodin at Sèvres.

F. B.

95

Portal of the Abbey Church of Saint-Pierre d'Auxerre

1881–1884

Pen and ink, brown ink wash on squared paper
H. 18.2 cm; W. 14.4 cm
D. 5916-5918

Rodin's passion for architecture, for France's Gothic churches in particular, and the emotion he felt when standing before these monuments from the past, before these "vibrant old stones", often mutilated and blackened, haunted him for over 40 years and regularly led him out onto the roads of Touraine and Anjou, or into the Indre valley and Burgundy… His first grand tour of the cathedrals of France was in 1877. He jotted down countless notes and drawings in small sketchbooks, which, in 1914, gave rise to the publication of the only book Rodin ever wrote, illustrated with 100 reproductions of his drawings, *Les Cathédrales de France* (Paris, Armand Colin, 1914).

This page, similar in style to his "black drawings" through his use of ink and dark washes and contrasting effects of light and shade, attests to the number of modest, small-scale sketches Rodin accumulated and to the fondness for detail that was evident in most of his architectural drawings – cornices, volutes, capitals, mouldings and doors retained his attention more than a building or its *façades* in their entirety. On this sheet, for example, the lower architectural detail possibly represents the western portal of the abbey church of Saint-Pierre d'Auxerre, while the upper drawing shows a detail from one of the side doors. Rodin's interest in this classic 17th-century church reveals how the sculptor's love of past architecture went far beyond the Gothic period.

N. L.

When Rodin received the commission for *The Gates of Hell* **(11-14)**, he immersed himself in Dante's *Divine Comedy*, "pencil in hand", and made over 100 drawings, which were not designs for the monument, but a means of "working in the spirit of this formidable poet", as he wrote in a letter to Léon Gauchez. Invaded by dark lines or ink washes, these sketches became known as the "black drawings", both because of the technique used and the infernal world they depict.

Among the desperate, endlessly wandering souls whom Dante and Virgil encounter during their journey, Ugolino was the one that especially fuelled Rodin's imagination. The artist decided to follow all the episodes of the count's tragic destiny, from his imprisonment in the Tower of Pisa, where he had been condemned to starve to death with his children, to the atrocious scenes in which he devoured his own sons.

In this pyramidal composition, the contorted bodies and screaming mouths are modelled by shadowy grey washes and white gouache highlights, while a mass of entangled lines in pencil or red ink confer a frenetic, bloodthirsty aspect on the scene. The turbulent, poignant nature of this image is heightened by the dark expression on the face of Ugolino, who, as his sons cling to his side, seeks to stifle a scream of terror with his left hand or to cover his ravenous mouth.

N. L.

96

Ugolino surrounded by his Three Children

Circa 1880

Pencil, pen and wash, ink
and gouache on paper
H. 17.3 cm; W. 13.7cm
Former Maurice Fenaille Collection,
acquired in 1929?
D. 5624

This work on paper is one of the gouache or ink wash drawings that Rodin did while reading Dante's *Divine Comedy*, in 1880-83.

The central figure, curled up on himself, immersed in a sort of cesspool, is literally drowning in violet ink, while a procession of shades seem to observe him from above. Annotated in pen and ink on the right, *dans la m…*, this drawing recalls the meeting between Dante and one of the corrupters and flatterers, Alessio Interminei of Lucca: "And I, thence peering down, saw people in the lake's foul bottom, plunged in dung… Searching its depths, I there made out a smeared head…" (Dante, *Inferno*, Canto XVIII).

In the S… illustrates a process frequently used by Rodin the draughtsman – collage. The drawing, made on a fragile page from a notebook of ordinary paper, was subsequently cut out by the artist and stuck onto a larger sheet of paper. The consolidation of the original drawing at the same time enabled it to be enlarged, extended. This practice demonstrates how Rodin refused to "finish" a work, to consider it final. He was in the habit of reworking earlier drawings and combining them with new sketches, or new figures, as part of a metamorphic, cyclic process that would later reoccur in his sculptures.

N. L.

97

In the S…

Circa 1880

Pencil, pen and ink, ink wash and gouache on paper mounted on ruled paper from a ledger
H. 18,2 cm; W. 13,6cm
Former Maurice Fenaille Collection, acquired in 1929?
D. 7616

98

Force and Ruse

Circa 1880

Pen and ink, wash and gouache on
paper pasted on a support mounted
on cardboard
H. 15.5 cm; W. 19.2 cm
D. 5087

Emerging from a vague universe of ink wash and gouache is a tormented drawing of raw beauty, representing the violence of a mythical coupling between a centaur and a woman. It is hard to distinguish whether what is depicted is the violence of an abduction or the fiery passion of a woman, ardently straddling the fabulous creature's rump.

Half-man, half-horse, the centaur, who represents the tumultuous battles between body and soul, between angel and beast, was one of Rodin's favourite themes in the 1870s. Springing from the artist's imagination, this work belongs to the period of his "black drawings", even if it does not illustrate an episode from Dante's *Hell*, but instead draws its inspiration from another of Rodin's preferred books, Ovid's *Metamorphoses*.

In this almost monochrome work featuring large, Michelangelesque bodies, the murky brown wash, mixed with gouache, conceals the lines drawn in pencil or ink, giving rise to a constant tension between form and haziness, intention and fate.

N. L.

Most of the drawings Rodin made in relation to his sculptures were not preparatory sketches, but drawings made after the sculptures once finished, generally as illustrations for a book or magazine article. This is the case here, since the present drawing, which borrows the pose of the sculpture *Eve*, dating from 1881, was initially meant to illustrate Émile Bergerat's *Enguerrande*, but would eventually be used in 1900 on the frontispiece of Victor Émile Michelet's *Contes Surhumains*.

When he made drawings after his sculptures, Rodin used a network of more or less dense hatchings that carved out light and shade in a manner borrowed from engraving. The patches of ink and areas where it has run, like the highly emphatic hatchings around the figure and on the arm and head of Eve, create a very Rembrandtesque chiaroscuro. The woman's face is hidden in shadow, whereas the light seems to concentrate on her rounded belly. In this drawing, Eve, the faceless sinner, becomes the "bearer" of future humanity.

N. L.

99

Eve

Circa 1884

Pen and black ink, brown ink wash, on paper
H. 25.4 cm; W. 18.7cm
Marcel Guérin Bequest, 1948
D. 7142

100

Victor Hugo,
Three-Quarter View

1884

Dry-point engraving, 4th state of 10
Engraved part: H. 22.2 cm; W. 15 cm
Acquired in 1991
G. 7750

101

Henry Becque, 1885

Dry-point engraving
Engraved part: H. 22.5 cm; W. 16 cm
G. 9343

Rodin was introduced to copperplate engraving, or, to be more precise, to etching and dry-point engraving, in 1881, by his friend Alphonse Legros, then living in London. Although he soon mastered the technique, he only explored 13 subjects in his engravings, but often printed a large number of successive states. During his lifetime, the engravings he made after his portrait busts enabled him to familiarize the public with his freestanding sculpture and earned him an excellent reputation as an engraver.

Rodin is known to have been unable to get Victor Hugo to sit for his portrait bust and had to surreptitiously sketch the great poet as he went about his everyday tasks. He executed the bust of the writer between February and April 1883, then made the dry-point engravings of front and three-quarter views after the finished portrait. His virtuoso use of dry-point produced superb effects of contrast between the deep, velvety blacks and the white of the page and made the modelling of Hugo's face particularly lively. Rodin infused the spontaneity of a sketch into this engraved portrait by arranging it on the page with another view, placed in a different position.

In the portrait of Henry Becque (1837-99), Rodin placed a front view and two profile views of the writer side by side in the same copperplate, thereby multiplying the angles from which the sitter was seen and making him revolve around the sheet, like a bust placed on a sculptor's turntable.

N. L.

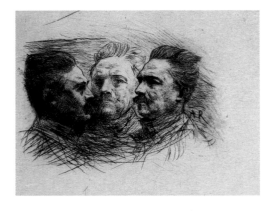

102

De Profundis Clamavi

1887-1888

Pen and brown ink, brown ink wash,
on a page from a copy of the original
edition of *Flowers of Evil*
H. 18.6cm; W. 12cm
Acquired by the Musée Rodin through
D. David-Weill and Maurice Fenaille,
1931
D. 7174 H

While Rodin stopped exploring the world of Dante and
drawings from his imagination in the
early 1880s, he remained faithful to
the highly contrasted style of his
"black drawings" **(96-98)** and continued to use gouache and ink wash
until the late 1880s.

The perpetuation of this style is particularly noticeable in some of the
ink drawings Rodin made for
Baudelaire's *Flowers of Evil*. Because
he felt a special affinity with the poet
and because he received a personal
commission from Paul Gallimard,
Rodin made 27 illustrations for the
publisher and book lover's own copy
of the work, between October 1887
and January 1888 **(194)**.

Derived from earlier drawings
inspired by Dante's *Inferno*, the pose
of these two lovers, whose bodies are
modelled by a few shadows in wash,
expresses all the pain and passion
contained in Baudelaire's verse,
which Rodin carefully copied onto
the bottom of the page: *page Cy/
j'implore ta pitié toi/ l'unique que
j'aime, du/ fond du gouffre obscur/ où
mon cœur est tombé (I do implore thy
pity, Thou whom alone I love/Deep in
this mournful vale wherein my heart is
fallen).*

N. L.

103

Two Women:
One helping the Other
to put on a Garment

Circa 1895

Pencil, ink, watercolour
and gouache on paper
H. 17.8 cm; W.11.7 cm
D. 4369

From the end of the 1880s, Rodin developed a new style of drawing, less sombre and less expressionistic than the "black drawings" that had dominated the early years of the decade. Circa 1890, after a phase in which he reduced his drawings to a few precise, fluid lines, Rodin increasingly made use of watercolour. As is shown here, he had a distinct preference for pinks and yellows, colours that clothe the bodies of his models, who were almost exclusively women.

The two women's rapidly sketched movements, the heavy, emphatic contour lines, like the vivid, arbitrary colours vying with the ink and pencil lines, were, for Rodin a means of portraying his figures on the spot, yet powerfully and expressively.

F. B.

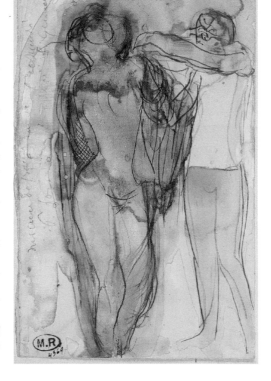

From 1890 onwards, as his reputation grew, the artist could at last afford to employ models on a regular basis. The female body, in all its many states, then became, with a few exceptions, his unique field of exploration. Forbidding any sort of pose, Rodin drew the model, asking her to move freely around his studio, and swiftly jotted down, with surprising vivacity, such and such a movement that seemed right or particularly expressive.

There is nothing academic about *Female Nude with Left Leg Outstretched*. It is a drawing devoid of modelling, with decidedly emphatic contours, sketched in pencil and ink, which make the silhouette in a *contrapposto* stance stand out against the white page. The time Rodin spent observing his model and executing his sketch was very brief. The insistent reworking of the contour lines and the amendments he made in strokes of red pastel attest to his desire to capture an authentic, expressive movement. This *Female Nude with Left Leg Outstretched* seems to herald the vitality of Fauvist drawings and the graphic investigations, circa 1903-06, of an artist like Matisse, who would write: "We strive to very rapidly discover what is characteristic about a gesture, an attitude. Didn't Delacroix say that we should be able to draw a man falling from a sixth floor window?" (Guenne, 1925).

N. L.

104

Female Nude with Left Leg Outstretched

Circa 1895

Pencil, ink and pastel on paper
H. 20.2 cm; W. 12.7 cm
D. 2165

105

Male Nude, with One Hand and Knee on the Ground

Circa 1896-1898

Pencil and watercolour on paper
H. 32.5 cm; L. 25 cm
D. 4181

Characteristic of the major change that occurred in Rodin's drawings from 1896, this sheet shows the artist's enthusiasm for "the sincere observation, which, disdaining theatrical poses, interests itself in the simple and much more touching attitudes of real life," (Gsell, 1911). From then on, Rodin only made drawings after a living model. He sought to capture chance movements, without taking his eyes off the model, without even glancing down at his sheet of paper.

In this rare pencil drawing of a male nude, the erratic, initial lines of this "snapshot of a movement" are still visible. Rodin subsequently re-worked and completed it with slashes of watercolour wash, a process Gsell described as follows: "The colouring of the flesh is dashed on in three or four broad strokes that score the torso and the limbs... These sketches fix the very rapid gesture or the transient motion which the eye itself has hardly seized for one half second. They do not give you merely line and colour: they give you movement and life," (Gsell, 1911).

N. L.

From 1900 onwards, when Rodin was particularly pleased with an attitude or movement in one or other of his drawings, he would sometimes cut it out to further experiment with it. He thus built up a stock of cut-out silhouettes, taken from his drawings. He would then select two or three of these figures and rearrange them in a new composition. Once he had decided on the arrangement, he would use tracing paper to transfer the composition onto another sheet of paper, to which he then applied watercolours. *Two Semi-Reclining Female Nudes* resulted from the assemblage of two such forms. Rodin emphasized the relief of the composition by passing one of the women's arms over the other one's legs.

Like all the cut-out paper figures in the museum collections, these were mounted on a support after the artist's death.

Rodin probably intended to use this two-figure assemblage in a new watercolour. The idea of replacing brushes and pencils with a pair of scissors would later be widely echoed, particularly in the Cubists' *papiers collés*, in the gouache-coloured paper cut-outs produced by Matisse in the last years of his life, and in the torn-up papers and drawings Jean Arp used as starting points for his *Constellations*, in the 1930s.

N. L.

106

Two Semi-Reclining Female Nudes

Circa 1900

Pencil and watercolour on paper, cut out and assembled
H. 32.6; W. 26.2 cm
D. 5192

107

Resurrection

Circa 1900

Pencil, watercolour and gouache
on paper
H. 49.9; W. 31.7 cm
D. 4692

As in his sculpture, Rodin experimented with combinations of figures in his drawings. This stunning composition thus resulted from the assemblage of two cut-out figures, probably traced from two separate drawings. As has been previously been seen, the two figures were then juxtaposed to give rise to a new work.

Through the addition of colour, Rodin then brought out the meaning he saw in this two-figure group. Applied in broad strokes of the brush thick with green, blue and purple gouache, the dark background seems to shrink back from the yellow halo that lights up the women's bodies. Like an angel, one of them touches the other with her right hand and thus appears to draw her out of the darkness and bring her back into the light of life.

The annotation *Resurrection*, later added by Rodin, confirms this interpretation of the work, but his fundamental preoccupation lay elsewhere; as always in Rodin's work, form was more important than subject, and the expressive force of the drawing alone sufficed.

F. B.

108

The Moon

Circa 1900

Pencil and watercolour on paper
H. 32.6 cm; W. 25 cm
D. 3968

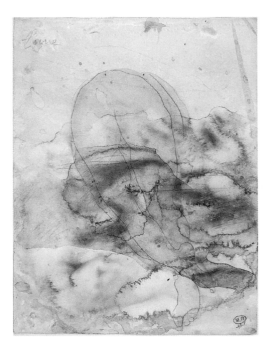

The watercolours Rodin executed from 1900 onwards helped establish his reputation as a draughtsman considerably. Here, a mix of subtle hues, ranging from ochre to violet, and diluted so as to form rings with jagged edges, creates a decidedly abstract space. Emerging from beneath these clouds of diffuse colours spreading out wherever chance carried them is a precise, continuous, fine line forming the buttocks and legs of a woman seen from behind. This synthetic, magnificently evocative, elliptical drawing undoubtedly stemmed from the subtle refinement of an earlier drawing, made in a few minutes, from life, after a model.

The patches of violet watercolour, in the centre, almost conceal the legs of the female nude; an ochre hue emphasizes and unifies the curve of the lower back, which seems to emerge from behind a thick mass of clouds, like a star.

N. L.

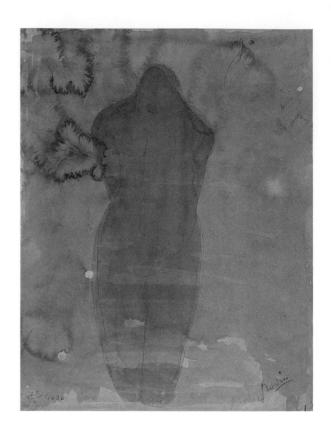

109

Rock

Circa 1900

Pencil and watercolour
on paper
H. 32.4 cm; W. 24.9 cm
D. 4636

A spiderlike continuous line, extremely fine, without any variation in thickness or sign of interruption, defines, against a blue watercolour background, the synthesized contour of a female nude, very slightly coloured in a brown ochre wash. The drawing did not spring from the artist's imagination but from his encounter with the real model. An attitude or a movement spontaneously captured could then be reworked, amended, pared down, enhanced with wash or watercolour, and repeated at will so as to create multiple variations on the same theme.

This was the case in this drawing of a kneeling woman with head thrown back, who borrows the form of an ancient vase and the colour of terracotta, to become one of the many versions of a "vase woman" invented by Rodin.

The blue watercolour engulfs the body of the naked woman in this drawing that Rodin called *Rock* and recalls, as in many of his works, the sensual and primordial universe of the ocean depths.

N. L.

110

Standing Embracing Couple, Profile View

Circa 1900

Pencil and watercolour on paper
H. 49.8 cm; W. 33 cm
D. 6203

The contrast between the treatment of the two bodies clasped in an embrace (whose fine pencil outlines are covered by a pale, flesh-coloured wash) and that of the flamboyant background against which they are set, and the clarity of the borders between human figures and background, recall the technique of collage. In fact, as is frequently found in Rodin's oeuvre, one work generated another, metamorphosed into a new composition.

In the present drawing, the artist seems to have traced an earlier drawing, probably the one entitled *A Reef at the Bottom of the Sea. Two Embracing Figures*, executed between 1896 and 1900, exhibited at the Pavillon de l'Alma, Paris, is now in the Weimar Museum. Then, using this tracing as a starting point, Rodin transferred the outline of the same couple onto a new sheet of paper, but here, the figures are not immersed in a watery universe as in the Weimar drawing, but stand out against a fiery background, streaked with vertical lines in pencil.

The abstract background, a sort of blood red stage curtain, removes all notion of temporality from this scene of two lovers fusing into one, which has no place in the tangible world.

N. L.

111

Slumber Flower. Young Mother embracing her Child

After 1900

Pencil and watercolour on paper
H. 25 cm; W. 32.5 cm
D. 4805

An ochre watercolour wash, brushed quickly across the woman's body, unifies the reclining figure and makes it stand out against the background. However, the wash does not remain within the outline and, as in many of Rodin's late watercolours, spreads over and beyond the pencil line, or, in places, forms cloudy patches or rings of diluted colour.

The drawing bears the sculptor's original annotation, *Fleur de sommeil*. But titles of Rodin's works were very often attributed and written down after the work was finished, sometimes even suggested by the people around him. For the artist, the title was secondary: "First of all, nature must be captured as it offers itself, then, once the work is finished, its precise meaning can be found, if one so wishes."

Rodin must have come back to this drawing and added a few strokes of thicker pencil, a base and a background to the slumbering woman. This was probably when the form of a tiny baby seemed to have emerged out of the patch of watercolour, beneath the sleeping nude's chin. He therefore made the lines clearer and completed the title with the addition of *Jeune mère embrasse son enfant*.

This work clearly shows how Rodin deliberately let himself be guided by the evocative power of a patch of colour, and incorporated chance into his creative process.

N. L.

112

Before the Creation

Circa 1900

Black pencil, stumping,
watercolour and gouache on paper
H. 25 cm; W. 32.5 cm
D. 6193

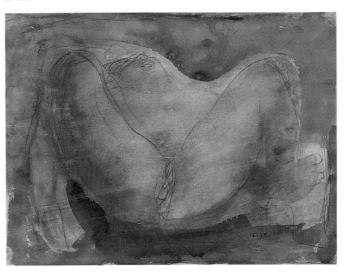

In Rodin's post-1900 oeuvre, the erotic drawings formed a body of several hundred works.

In his erotic drawings, Rodin always concentrated on one or two nude models, eagerly observing the mysterious regions of their genitalia. The naked women whom he sketched agreed to reveal, to expose their pudenda to his gaze, often caressing themselves, sometimes casting off all restraint... thus allowing the artist to capture the most intimate and most expressive movements of their bodies.

In the foreground of the composition of this watercolour drawing, annotated by Rodin, lower right, *avant la création*, a woman's vulva, exposed to view by her outspread thighs and the position of the foreshortened body, is the very subject of the drawing. On the face, anonymous and obscured by the way in which Rodin chose to frame his composition, the elliptical strands of hair and open mouth mirror and are aligned with the woman's genitalia. It is hard not to make an allusion to Courbet's *The Origin of the World* (1866), a picture that "appears as the ultimate point of the Realist conquest achieved by the painter" (Des Cars, 2007). In Rodin's work, however, the very "modern" assertion of a plastic vocabulary independent of reality (free handling, elliptical forms, intense colours, abstract background against which the naked body exposes itself, outside of any context) competes with the highly-charged eroticism of the drawing.

N. L.

113

Torso of a Reclining Female Nude, with one Hand on her Chest

After 1900

Pencil and stumping on paper
H. 20 cm; W. 31 cm
D. 2909

In the last years of his life, Rodin no longer contented himself with single line drawings, in fine dry pencil, covered with a light wash. He worked on the modelling with stumping, using his finger to crush a soft lead pencil to cloud over, or partially obliterate the pencil marks, to obtain hazier areas, with less contrast between the figure and the background. This return to a more naturalistic modelling is typical of Rodin's late drawings.

Parallels can be drawn between the more or less pronounced *sfumato*, or misty unfinished effects, and the handling of the marbles, where figures gently emerge out of an indistinct background and echo the hazy monochrome paintings of Rodin's great friend, Eugène Carrière.

N. L.

114

Salammbo

Circa 1900
Pencil and stumping on paper
H. 20.4 cm; W. 31 cm
D. 6012

In this drawing of a woman with outspread thighs, exposing her genitals, arching her back and hiding her face under her folded arms, the eroticism is highly charged. This body in a state of ecstasy is even more provocative because the artist, as in many of the drawings of his final years, used stumping to model the female form and infuse it with a sculptural presence.

The two annotations, *Salambô* and *St antoine (sic)*, make reference to Gustave Flaubert's eponymous nov-els. Without being an illustration for either of these books, this drawing, like others inscribed with the name Salammbo, attests to Rodin's admiration for the writer. As in most of Rodin's drawings, the titles are known to have been attributed by the artist a posteriori. The sensual character of this nude recalls some disturbing seduction scene that could be found either in the violent, exotic novel *Salammbo*, or in *The Temptation of Saint Anthony*.

N. L.

115

Cambodian Dancer

1906

Pencil and gouache on paper
H. 31.3 cm; W. 19.8 cm
D. 4428

On 10 July 1906, Rodin, aged 66, attended a performance given in the Pré-Catelan, Paris, by a troupe of Cambodian dancers, who had accompanied King Sisowath of Cambodia on his official visit to France. Enthralled by the beauty of these dancers and the novelty of their movements, Rodin followed them to Marseilles to be able to make as many drawings of them as possible before they left the country on 20 July.

They made a deep impression on the artist, as he confided to Georges Bourdon, in an article for the newspaper *Le Figaro* on 1 August 1906: "There is an extraordinary beauty, a perfect beauty, about these slow, monotonous dances, which follow the pulsating rhythm of the music… [The Cambodians] have taught me movements I had never come across anywhere before…" Rodin used gouache (ochre for the graceful arms and head, deep blue for the tunic draping the body), applied in broad brush strokes over and beyond the contour lines, to amend and rectify the initial pencil drawing of this crouching dancer's hieratic pose. All the details are eliminated (garments, face, hairstyle…). All that remains is the concentrated energy of the graceful, eloquent, age-old gestures. "In short," concluded Rodin, "if they are beautiful, it is because they have a natural way of producing the right movements…"

N. L.

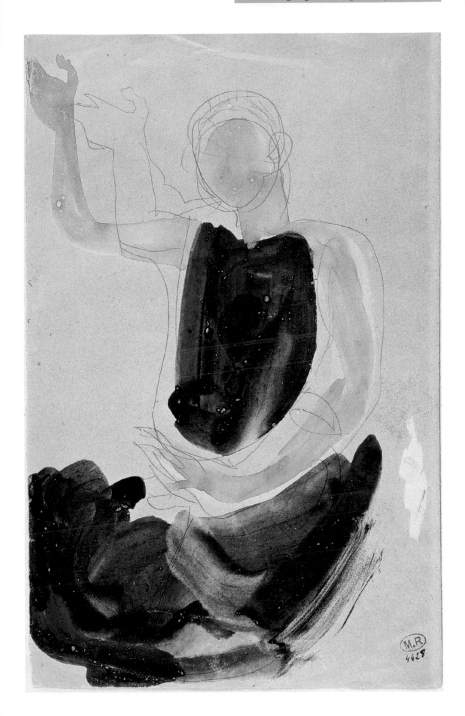

116

Cambodian Dancer

July 1906

Pencil, stumping, watercolour, gouache
soft lead pencil highlights on paper
H. 34.8 cm; W. 26.7 cm
D. 4455

On the subject of the Cambodian dancers – the novelty and perfection of whose movements elated and moved him profoundly – Rodin spoke with remarkably piercing insight:

"…They have even found a new movement, of which I was unaware: the jolts their body gives as it moves downward. And then their great strength lies in the fact that they keep their legs permanently bent, like a spring box, from which they can bounce or rise upwards as they wish, make themselves taller, at any given moment. It is a movement all of their own, unknown in the Antique and to us: when the arms are stretched out in the shape of a cross, they make a movement that snakes from one hand to the other, via the shoulder blades. This unknown, hitherto-unseen movement belongs to the Far East, i.e. when the movement of the left arm forms a concave curve, the other forms a convex curve, and they bring these arms into play, in a movement that darts past the shoulder blades." (Judrin, 2002).

N. L.

117

Hanako

1907

Pencil on paper
H. 30.9 cm; W. 19.5 cm
D. 1141

This work on paper is one of the countless drawings sketched from life by Rodin, without taking his eyes off the model.

It is easy to recognize in this figure the Japanese actress Hanako **(76)**, whom Rodin met in Marseilles in 1906. Fascinated by the expressivity of her face, the sculptor persuaded her to come and pose for him. He modelled 58 sculptures of Hanako, as well as a large number of drawings, made in a single sitting, during which he sought to capture her exceptional energy on his sheets of paper.

Rodin was struck by the powerful muscles of this tiny dancer's "exotic" body, as he told Paul Gsell: "She is so strong that she can stand as long as she wants on one leg, while lifting the other in front of her at a right angle. She thus appears to be rooted to the ground like a tree…" (Gsell, 1911).

N. L.

118

Astarte, after the Dancer Alda Moreno

Circa 1912

Pencil and stumping
H. 20.1 cm; W. 31 cm
D 2830

Seldom can Rodin's models be identified. Circa 1910, he made the acquaintance of a Spanish dancer and acrobat working at the Opéra Comique, called Alda Moreno, the forms of whose athletic body can be seen in about 50 drawings. These superb line drawings, on sheets larger than those Rodin ordinarily used, were executed in pencil and stumped so as to model the volumes of the body more accurately.

The inscription, *Astarté*, made by Rodin to the acrobat's right, identifies the female body with a star. Astarté or Ishtar, the daughter of the moon god and the twin sister of the sun, was worshipped as the goddess of Love and Desire in Mesopotamian mythology and assimilated to Aphrodite by the Greeks.

In this drawing, the dancer, whose acrobatic pose recalls a yoga position, seems to be hovering over the ground, rather like a flying saucer. The litheness of her body is accentuated by the excessive stretching movement of the supple arm. The extension of and amendments to the fingers touching the edge of the sheet, like the word *bas* inscribed by the artist on the right, illustrate Rodin's habit of turning his drawings around to find a new direction for them, a new meaning.

N. L.

119

Two Woman Embracing

1908

Pencil and watercolour on paper
H. 32 cm; W. 24 cm
D. 7195

The theme of Sapphic love frequently recurred in the drawings of Rodin, who often employed several models at the same time.

The impetuosity and accuracy of the movement must have been captured spontaneously, then transferred onto another sheet, since Rodin was in the habit of tracing his initial drawing to obtain another, more refined one. This was the process used in the present drawing, where the contour bears no sign of error or correction. The magnificently controlled, unbroken line defines and models the forms, which have become timeless, which are not even concealed by the usual daub of pale ochre wash. The only colours are in the splotch of blue watercolour on the folds of the drapery of the woman on the left and the dabs of yellow ochre highlighting the hair.

This work epitomizes the duality between the immediacy of real facts and the search for style in Rodin's drawings. It is also exceptional because of the dedication: *Hommage/à ma grande amie/Judith Cladel/Auguste Rodin/1908.* Judith Cladel, the sculptor's unfailing supporter, was the first person to classify the Musée Rodin's large collection of drawings after his death.

N. L.

2. OTHER COLLECTIONS

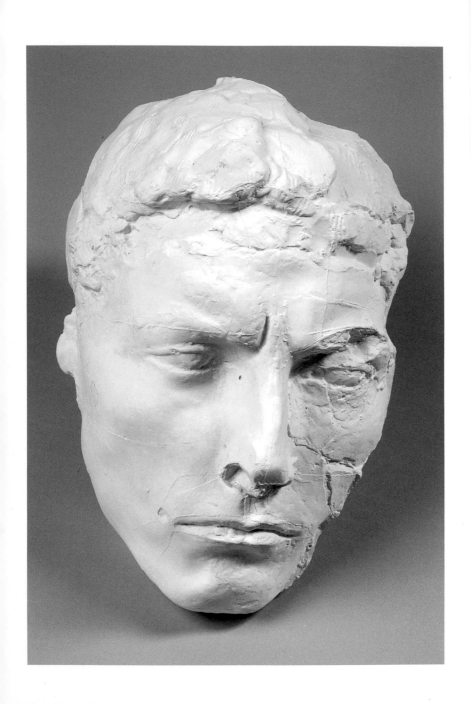

Nadine LEHNI, Aline MAGNIEN, Aurore MÉCHAIN

Rodin's circle

mongst its collections, the Musée Rodin boasts some 200 paintings, 500 drawings, over 1,000 prints and 164 sculptures by other artists, most of whom were Rodin's contemporaries. These works were acquired by the sculptor during his lifetime. They do not really form a coherent collection, for the acquisition of a certain number of these works, given to Rodin or exchanged with one of his sculptures, often appears to be the fruit of chance rather than the outcome of a collector's impassioned and focused choice.

However, it is obvious that Rodin took a lively interest in the artists of his day. He especially liked to exhibit his sculptures opposite a painter's works and showed his admiration for some of these artists by modelling their portrait busts or designing a monument in their memory (Dalou, Legros, Jean-Paul Laurens, Falguière, Puvis de Chavannes, James Whistler…). Also in this collection are a number of portraits of Rodin (notably by Antoine Bourdelle, Camille Claudel, Jean-Paul Laurens, John Singer Sargent and Eugène Carrière), some of which were exchanged for a sculpture.

Rodin's friendships and tastes led to him surrounding himself with works by the Naturalists (Théodule Ribot, Alfred Roll, Jules Bastien-Lepage, Fritz Thaulow…) and Symbolists (Eugène Carrière, Charles Cottet…). While the Neo-Impressionists, the Nabis and the Fauves are not represented in his collection, the sculptor did, however, purchase three Van Goghs (including *Père Tanguy*, late 1887), Renoir's *Nude in the Sunlight*, and Monet's *Belle-Île*, which are true masterpieces. Through a series of exchanges made with his friend of almost 20 years, Rodin also owned eight paintings by Eugène Carrière, who shared the sculptor's fondness for unfinished works. Rodin seldom collected pieces by contemporary sculptors and they rarely dared to make him a gift of their works except in portrait form. If the museum now has a large collection of Camille Claudel's works — and probably some of her finest sculptures, assembled since 1951 in a room that bears her name — they were acquired later through purchases and donations,

ANTOINE
BOURDELLE
(1861-1929)
Mask of Apollo
1898-1899
S. 2842

notably by her brother, the writer Paul Claudel. It is therefore worth underlining the rare occasions on which Rodin deliberately decided to acquire a sculpture (from Aristide Maillol, Jules Desbois) or exchange one of his own for another work (by Medardo Rosso, Constantin Meunier).

The exchanges he made with Rosso, Maillol or Meunier are known to have been based on mutual admiration. He regarded Maillol as one of the finest sculptors of his generation and is supposed to have named Jules Desbois as his successor, shortly before his death, "After me, Desbois will be the greatest sculptor".

N. L./A. M.

120

JULES DESBOIS (1851-1935)

Misery

After 1887

Terracotta
H. 37,5 cm; W. 17,7 cm; D. 24,6 cm
Gift of Mme G. Rudier, 1954
S. 1150

Jules Desbois was Cavelier's pupil and Rodin's assistant. The present terracotta was cast from the original, shown in plaster at the Paris Salon in 1894, and then reworked. This cast does not seem to be unique and Desbois, probably influenced by Rodin, made several working versions of it.

Misery itself was produced in different media and different sizes. The themes of old age and *memento mori* epitomized in the figure belong to a longstanding sculptural tradition, which Desbois interprets here. Rodin and Camille Claudel also handled this subject in *She Who Was the Helmet Maker's Once-Beautiful Wife* (31) and *Clotho* (123), respectively, and apparently used the same model, an elderly Italian woman called Maria Caira. This sculptural jousting between artists who were very close and who respected each other profoundly shows that, beyond the evident lifelikeness of the work, art, not nature, was what was really at stake here. A sculpture of such a body was an anatomical study as well as an artistic challenge, in which the ugliness of the knotty muscles, the emaciated limbs and the wrinkled skin should give rise to emotion and beauty.

A. M.

121

CONSTANTIN MEUNIER (1831–1905)

The Glassblower

1889

Bronze, cast by J. Petermann, Brussels
H. 54.5 cm; L. 18.3 cm; D. 14.2 cm
S. 3071

Meunier was one of the leading Belgian artists of his day. He turned to sculpture after trying his hand at painting. His work focused mainly on the depiction of working people. Like Aimé-Jules Dalou (1838-1902), in particuliar, he was sensitive to the emotion, dignity and sombre beauty that emanated from the figures of manual workers whom he portrayed on several occasions. Compared to Michelangelo because of the power exuding from his sculptures, he infused these subjects with a force echoed in literature by Zola, whose characters also had an innate sense of tragic dignity and strength.

As was customary, especially where Rodin was concerned, the work was given by the artist to the French sculptor, after the first Salon de la Société Nationale des Beaux-Arts, in 1890, in exchange for a small group called *Women Embracing*.

In France, Rodin's support was important for Meunier's career. They both readily used exaggerated proportions to better indicate the strength of manual workers' hands or ploughmen's "colossal" backs, or the attitudes shaped by labourers' tasks. Portrayed here is a glassblower, a skilled craftsman, an aristocrat among ordinary working men.

A. M.

122

MEDARDO ROSSO (1858-1928)

Laughing Girl also known as *Small Laughing Girl*

1890

H. 37 cm; W. 20 cm; D. 26 cm
Bronze and onyx
Inscribed: *Rosso a Rodin*
S. 528

Medardo Rosso, a sculptor from Milan who settled in Paris between 1885 and 1890, made friends with Eugène Carrière (1849-1906) and Rodin, before breaking off relations with the latter after his *Balzac* **(52)** was unveiled in 1898, when he accused the French sculptor of intellectual theft and plagiary. In 1893, Rosso had exchanged *Laughing Girl* for the torso known as the *Petit-Palais Torso*. The present work is an expressive head, not the portrait of an operetta singer, Bianca Caravaglia, supposedly from Toledo, even if the choice of the model reflected both Rosso's love of the theatre and a longstanding iconographic tradition. Among the numerous versions, the Musée Rodin bronze highlights the physiognomy through the simplicity of its presentation on an onyx base. Fleeting in essence, laughter modifies the facial features and, helped by the inner and outer light, reveals a different face. This concept fascinated both the artist and his era. Rosso's characteristic soft, hazy modelling, often compared to Impressionist painting, also conveys these facial dynamics.

A. M.

123

CAMILLE CLAUDEL (1864–1943)

Clotho

1893

Plaster
H. 90 cm; W. 49.3 cm; D. 43 cm
S. 1379

Exhibited at the Paris Salon in 1893, this work drew its inspiration from Greco-Roman mythology. An appeal fund launched in 1895 to pay tribute to Puvis de Chavannes enabled a marble version to be commissioned from the artist. Completed in 1897 and shown at the Salon in 1899, the marble has unfortunately been lost.

Clotho was the youngest of the Three Fates who decided human destiny. Shown here as a very elderly woman, the sculpture forms part of Rodin and Claudel's artistic dialogue about the depiction of old age. Rodin had tackled this theme in 1884–85, in *She Who Was the Helmet Maker's Once-Beautiful Wife* **(31)**; his assistant, Jules Desbois, had used the same model for his terracotta *Misery* in 1894 **(120)**. The work may also be seen as a reference to Claudel's preoccupation with destiny, other signs of which are evident in her work.

Ensnared in her hair that weighs so heavily on her head and seems to paralyze her, *Clotho*, shown at the Salon at the same time as *The Waltz*, is almost its exact antithesis.

A. M.

124

CAMILLE CLAUDEL (1864–1943)

The Gossips
or Women Chatting

1897

Onyx marble and bronze
H. 45 cm; W. 42.2 cm; D. 39 cm
S. 1006

In a letter dated 1893 to her brother Paul, Claudel mentions a small group of three women listening to another, all seated behind a screen. Possibly inspired by a scene she had observed in a railway carriage, *The Gossips* was exhibited in the plaster version at the Paris Salon in 1895. Two years later, an onyx and bronze version was also shown at the Salon. Two other versions of the same work, in marble and bronze, marble or plaster, exist in public and private collections.

Presented as a *Life Study*, the title given to the exhibit at the Salon in 1895, it is one of Claudel's most original works. In the Musée Rodin version, the emphasis is on the preciousness of the materials used and the Japanese influence at play in this group of women, whose attitudes may suggest a meeting of meddling gossips, but whose nudity, hair and slightly protrusive jaws suggest something far different. In some versions, their hair tends to become a quasi-independent object, which only heightens the strangeness of this nevertheless familiar scene.

A. M.

125

Camille Claudel
(1864-1943)

The Wave
or *The Bathers*

1897
Onyx marble and bronze,
1898-1903
H. 62 cm; W. 56 cm; D. 50 cm
Purchased by the museum,
1995
S. 6659

Shown in its plaster version at the Salon in 1897, *The Wave*, like *The Gossips* (124), was made almost entirely by Camille Claudel herself. The three identical small female figures all bend their knees at the sight of the huge wave of onyx marble about to break over their heads. It may be seen as an image of destiny, as found in several other works by the artist during this period.

Stylistically, the choice of semi-precious materials, like onyx marble, shows Claudel's affinity with Charles Cordier and with her contemporaries' attraction to play of colour and the natural polychromy of materials. Here the bronze dialogues with the greens of the stone.

Influenced by Japanese art, similar in colour and form to Hokusai's famous woodblock print, *The Wave* is a decorative work that gives priority to light and heralds Claudel's later series – her *Chimney-pieces (Deep Thought, Fireside Dream)* – in which the combinations of materials play such a fundamental role.

A. M.

126

CAMILLE CLAUDEL (1864-1943)

The Age of Maturity or *Destiny* or *The Path of Life* or *Fatality.*

1899

Bronze, cast by Frédéric Carvilhani,
after 1913, title and signature on the base
H. 121 cm; W. 181.2 cm; D. 73 cm
Gift of Paul Claudel, 1952
S. 1380

The first version of *The Age of Maturity*, only a plaster of which is in our possession, dates from 1894-95 according to a letter sent by Claudel to her brother Paul, in December 1893, where she calls it her "three-figure group". The sculptress envisaged including a tree leaning at an angle in the group to further underline her central idea of destiny.

The second version was commissioned by the French state in 1895, but although it was completed and paid for in 1898, it was never delivered by the artist. The first cast was made for a private client, Captain Tissier (Musée d'Orsay), and the plaster is thought to have been lost

when the second bronze was cast by Carvilhani in 1913. Often interpreted as an autobiographical work, illustrating Rodin hesitating between his ageing mistress and his young lover, the very well-constructed sculpture above all appears as a variation on the theme of destiny. In the first version, the man is still held firmly by youth and life, whereas in the second version, unable to resist being led away, he is pulled from the outstretched arms of the young imploring woman by old age and death. The tormented drapery and strong use of shadow show the influence of Art Nouveau aesthetics on this second version.

A. M.

127

CAMILLE CLAUDEL (1864–1943)

Vertumnus and Pomona

1905

White marble on red marble base
H. 91 cm; W. 80.6 cm; D. 41.8 cm
Signed on the back of the base:
Camille Claudel
Entitled: *Vertumnus and Pomona*
S. 1293

This sculpture was executed in various media and was given various titles. Inspired by an Indian play about Sakuntala's reunion with her husband after a long separation caused by a magic spell, the work was first modelled in plaster circa 1886. After repeated requests for a state commission and Claudel's crushed hopes, the work was finally carved in marble thanks to the Comtesse de Maigret in 1905. At his point, it was entitled *Vertumnus and Pomona*. The bronze, cast by Eugène Blot, was shown the same year at the Salon d'Automne under the title *Abandon*. The subject thus moved from Hindu to Greek mythology, then onto psychology or personal history.

The variations between the different versions bear witness to the investigations pursued by the artist. The change of title, combined with the change of medium, attest to this variety of interpretations and meanings which also formed part of her research.

A. M.

128

ARISTIDE MAILLOL
(1861-1944)

Woman with a Chignon
or The Bather

1900
Babbitt metal?
H. 67 cm; W. 15 cm; D. 15 cm
S. 579

The work seems to have been made out of Babbitt metal, an alloy of tin or lead and antimony, an inexpensive metal used in casting as a replacement for bronze, sometimes called "the poor man's bronze". Purchased by Rodin in 1904 for 500 francs from Ambroise Vollard, the art dealer who was promoting Maillol at this time, *The Bather* appealed to the sculptor because of its extremely smooth modelling "without blacks".

The two artists had great respect for each other. While Rodin was "the god of sculpture" in Maillol's eyes, the master saw a search for eternity in the younger sculptor's works, which placed *The Bather* or *Woman with a Chignon* on a par with the archaic statues being rediscovered during this period. Maillol's forms were no doubt influenced by Gauguin and his full, smooth, serene figures. What Rodin himself was seeking, especially in his late career, was something close to Maillol's compact, simplified forms. This new canon, quite unlike classical sculpture, is also found in Rodin's oeuvre, but the sensuality emanating from Maillol's works is more serene and peaceful than in Rodin's sculptures.

A. M.

129

ANTOINE BOURDELLE

Portrait of Rodin

"Au maître Rodin.
Ces profils rassemblés"

1910

Bronze
H. 89.5 cm; W. 63 cm; D. 61.8 cm
Rhodia Dufet-Bourdelle Donation, 1996
S. 6675

Exhibited at the Salon in 1910, this totemic portrait bust or terminal figure gave rise to considerable perplexity. The first version was even more puzzling: it emphasized the impression of the sculptor being cramped in a taller sheath, while two small horns, emerging out of his crew cut, projected a powerfully creative, faunlike image of Rodin. Dictated by feelings of immense admiration, the present work is a fervent tribute which thus deifies the master, while the subtitle highlights one of his contributions to sculpture: his theory of profiles. According to this theory, truth is attained through "the dense execution of profiles" and the work "expresses itself". By condensing distinguishing features and generalities in the portrait, again applying the lessons learned from Rodin, Bourdelle produced a veritable icon here.

A. M.

130

Eugène Carrière (1849–1906)

Woman combing her Hair seen from Behind

Circa 1889

Oil on canvas
H. 56 cm; W. 46.5 cm
P. 7275

Rodin probably met Eugène Carrière circa 1885 through the critic Roger Marx. Their friendship lasted until the painter's death – Carrière was notably one of Rodin's supporters during the *Balzac* affair in 1898 – and went hand in hand with a deep respect for each other's works. The two friends regularly visited one another's studios and their mutual admiration gradually led to them exchanging some of their works. This is why the Musée Rodin today has 11 canvases by the painter in its collections. *Woman combing her Hair seen from Behind* attests to Carrière's interest in the depiction of the female body, an interest he shared with Rodin. There is an intimate dialogue between the forms modelled by the sculptor out of a raw material and the painter's evanescent figures, with hazy contours hovering between light and shade. The handling of the light, characteristic of Carrière's works, envelops and enhances the model's flesh. The spectator's gaze is thus guided to the painting's most essential element: the body of this woman combing her hair.

Au. M.

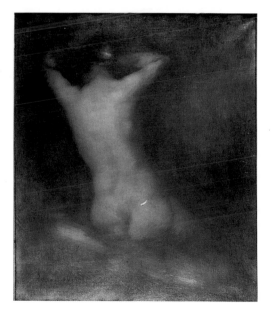

131

CHARLES COTTET (1863-1924)

Seascape

1903

Oil on card
H. 47 cm; W. 66 cm
P. 7288

Charles Cottet is regarded as the leader of the "black group", a movement that developed parallel to the Nabis. He rubbed shoulders with numerous artists, including Rodin, who acquired this painting when visiting his friend's studio. The Musée Rodin has three canvases by Cottet in its collections. Like many of the artists of his day, the painter was interested in depicting Breton life. But whereas his contemporaries sought a picturesque Brittany, painted in the open air, Cottet recre-ated his landscapes in the studio, by synthesizing different views. *Seascape* is one of these views transposed from reality. No human figures are included. The painter preferred to depict nature beneath a stormy sky. Playing with atmospheric effects and variations in the sky, he produced a work with realist undertones, in which the sea offers a glimpse of its potential brutality.

Au. M.

132

Alexandre Falguière (1831–1900)

Seated Diana

1878
Oil on canvas
H. 160.5 cm; W. 125 cm
P. 7297

Falguière and Rodin were firm friends. "The *Balzac* affair", during which Rodin would lose the commission from the Société des Gens de Lettres to Falguière, would have no impact on the quality of their relationship. Rodin, who regarded Falguière as a great artist, purchased this *Seated Diana*, in spite of its poor condition, after his friend's death to help his widow financially. It is a preparatory study for a painting exhibited at the Salon in 1879. Frequently represented by artists since the Renaissance, the scene shows a pensive Diana, with a shapely, expressive body. Her forms are statuesque. To break away from the monumentality of his figure, the painter introduced the colour red, which confers an expressive quality on the work. Falguière tackled his canvas like a sculptor: he scratched the paint away, reworked it, revealing his talent as a colourist and thus showing how closely painting and sculpture interact in his work.

Au. M.

133

CLAUDE MONET (1840–1926)

Belle-Île

1886

Oil on canvas
H. 65 cm; W. 85.5 cm
P. 7329

M onet and Rodin not only admired each other professionally but were also close friends. Their works were shown together in 1889 at a joint exhibition held at the Galerie Georges Petit. In 1888, Monet apparently gave this painting to the sculptor in exchange for his *Young Mother in the Grotto* **(28)**. *Belle-Île* belongs to a series of 39 canvases painted by Monet during a long visit to Belle-Île-en-Mer in 1886. For ten weeks, he wandered around the wildest part of the island. He set up his easel along the jagged coastline to paint in the open air and capture the infinite variations of light.

Influenced by the Japanese artist Hokusai's prints, he painted numerous views of rocks in the sea without any human presence and, while gazing at the immensity of the surrounding ocean, injected new life into his own pictorial language. The canvases painted on Belle-Île represented a turning point in Monet's career, for this was the beginning of the work on series that he undertook from the 1890s onwards: observing the metamorphosis of a motif at different times of day and year, a process which then became systematic and would epitomize his oeuvre for ever.

Au. M.

134

EDVARD MUNCH (1863-1944)

Rodin's "Thinker" in Dr Linde's Garden in Lübeck

Circa 1907

Oil on canvas
H. 122 cm; W. 78 cm
P. 7612

In 1905, Dr Linde, a well-informed German collector, purchased an enlarged bronze cast of *The Thinker* (**68**) from Rodin to adorn the garden of his home in Lübeck. At the same time, he struck up a friendship with Edvard Munch, from whom he commissioned several works in order to help him financially.

Linde soon drew parallels between the works of these two artists. He saw their shared desire to push back the limits of artistic representation. *Rodin's "Thinker" in Dr Linde's Garden in Lübeck* was painted by the artist shortly before he suffered a nervous breakdown in October 1908. The colour applied in crosshatchings is characteristic of this period in Munch's career, when his depression had not yet fully declared itself. The flat treatment of the sky and trees, which frame the scene, contrasts with the thickness of the paint on Mrs Linde's white silhouette that acts as an echo to *The Thinker.*

Au. M.

135

AUGUSTE RENOIR (1841–1919)

Nude in the Sunlight

Circa 1880

Oil on canvas
H. 81.4 cm; W. 64.9 cm
P. 7334

Rodin believed that Van Gogh and Renoir were the two greatest painters of their generation. The sculptor was particularly attached to this painting that he was able to purchase from Bernheim-Jeune in 1910, but which he had wanted since 1898. It dates from the period when Renoir, heedful of Ingres and Raphael's teachings, began distancing himself from Impressionism and giving priority back to line and contours. Handled like a sketch, this seated young woman attests to the distinctive sculptural qualities found in the painter's finest nudes. The visible juxtaposed dabs of pure colour form a sort of halo, or mandorla, around the voluptuous female nude. The soft modelling of the body seems to have emerged out of a hazy background, establishing an effect of contrast that could not fail to please Rodin. A photograph taken at the time shows the painting hanging on the wall – a rare occurrence – above Rodin's desk in the Hôtel Biron. The sculptor loved to show it to people and comment upon it: "The torso of this young woman is pure sculpture. What a marvel!" (Tirel, 1923).

"Look at this *Nude* by Renoir, look at the quality of this flesh; it shines in the night: it's a real Praxiteles!" (Revers, 1911).

N. L.

136

JOHN SINGER SARGENT (1856-1925)

Portrait of Rodin

1884
Oil on canvas
H. 72 cm; W. 53 cm
P. 7341

After serving an apprenticeship with the society painter Carolus-Duran from 1874 to 1878, Sargent gained widespread recognition as a portraitist and developed a complex style that was at once sophisticated and theatrical. In 1884, Sargent and Rodin, both foreign artists invited to the Salon des Vingt in Brussels, became friends. That same year, the painter executed this portrait of Rodin.

Sargent presents a singular image of the sculptor, devoid of any allusion to his profession. All attention is focused on his face, which looms out of the darkness. Sporting a thick beard, the sitter reveals a strong personality. The leonine significance of this beard and hair is combined with the painter's determination to render the sculptor's expression gentle and piercing. Here, Sargent's virtuosity lies in his ability to produce a portrait of both Rodin's physical features and intellect.

Au. M.

R odin probably met Fritz Thaulow in 1892, when the Norwegian painter settled in France with his family. As a token of their friendship, Rodin gave Thaulow several works, including a *Head of Saint John the Baptist*. Moved by this gesture, the painter, in turn, gave Rodin two canvases: *Small Town Square* (possibly Place du Moulin à vent, Dieppe) and *Factories in the Snow*.

Born into a wealthy family, Thaulow could afford to travel all over Europe. He took advantage of the journeys he made to paint in the open air and increase the number of his subjects. *Small Town Square* attests to his constant search for new motifs. In it, the painter captures a moment in the life of a small French town and depicts two figures seen from behind, under the moonlight. The scene is both fleeting and anonymous. Here, Thaulow shows that he has adopted Impressionist theories, making light and its fleeting variations his principal concern.

Au. M.

137

FRITZ THAULOW (1847-1906)

Small Town Square

Circa 1896

Oil on canvas
H. 73 cm; W. 92 cm
P. 7344

138

VINCENT VAN GOGH (1853-1890)

Père Tanguy

1887

Oil on canvas
H. 92 cm; W. 75 cm
P. 7302

Having said goodbye to his native Brabant and his early religious vocation, Van Gogh joined his brother Theo in Paris, in March 1886. This was where he met one of the most delightful characters in the Parisian art world of the 1880s, the man his painter friends affectionately called "Père Tanguy". Julien-François Tanguy (1825-94) ran a small paint supplies shop, on the Rue Clauzel, and often accepted paintings in exchange for the goods he sold.

Van Gogh painted three portraits of Père Tanguy, whose friendship he valued enormously. In this work, with which the shopkeeper never parted, the pure colours, the use of contrasting complementary colours, the visible, well-positioned brushwork and the flat picture space are all features of a Neo-Impressionist style that the artist used very freely. He chose to represent the old man in a strictly frontal pose, immobile, lost in thought, with his hands clasped over his stomach, and succeeded in capturing all the sitter's kindness and modesty. Van Gogh paid homage to the "colour grinder" by turning him into a sort of Japanese sage, placed against a background filled with some of the countless brightly coloured Japanese prints that the painter and his brother Theo collected.

From 1887, Rodin could also admire the writer Edmond de Goncourt's Japanese prints. The sculptor himself built up a private collection of prints, comparable to those of Monet and Van Gogh. Did Rodin purchase this major work of art in 1894 because he and Van Gogh shared a love of Japanese art? In any case, the sculptor bought two other important paintings of his and frequently spoke of his admiration for Vincent Van Gogh, whom he regarded as "an admirable demolisher of academic formulae, [who] also had a genius for light," (Rodin, 1909).

N. L.

139

VINCENT VAN GOGH (1853–1890)

The Harvesters

Late June–July 1888

Oil on canvas
H. 73 cm; W. 54 cm
P. 7304

This painting by Van Gogh is closely related to Provence, where the artist spent the last three years of his life. On arriving in Arles in February 1888, he was amazed by the light that made all the colours so intense. In this picture, the view from above, which places the horizon line very high up and reduces the sky to a thin band, enables the golden wheat field and sheaves, gleaming in the summer heat, to occupy almost the entire canvas. In the upper part of the painting, between the edge of the field and the bluish profile of the town of Arles, the long silhouette of a train can be seen puffing clouds of steam that echo the smoke from the factory chimneys, in the distance, on the left. This tranquil incorporation of modernity and progress into rural occupations and landscapes reflects the attraction Impressionist painters felt for the power and poetry of the railways, in the 1870s. The juxtaposed strokes of paint carefully applied in a specific direction, the brilliant, expressive colours and thick, frenzied brushwork, which are all characteristic of Van Gogh's late period, are governed here by a bedazzled, sun-drenched vision.

Purchased from Amédée Schuffenecker, after 1905, this painting was particularly treasured by the sculptor: "Van Gogh and Renoir are the two greatest painters of our time," he confided to Canudo. "The former's landscapes, the latter's nudes, have been so glorified that one should learn a great deal from their art..." (Canudo, 1913).

N. L.

D. Freuler. *Rodin working
from a Bare-Chested Model.*
Ph. 2005

Photography

The Musée Rodin has approximately 25,000 photographs, but only 7,000 of them were collected by Rodin himself. The subjects and themes are varied: the personal albums attest to his centres of interest and artistic sources, while the portraits and newspaper photographs illustrate his life. These photographs above all record what happened in the studio, between 1877 and 1917, the year the sculptor died.

Rodin employed professional photographers, some of whom have been forgotten today, such as Gaudenzio Marconi, Charles Michelez, Charles Bodmer and Victor Pannelier, as well as amateurs like Eugène Druet and Jean Limet. Rodin used the pictures taken by these photographers to study the gestation of a work, to amend it first in pencil, then in three dimensions. By having a picture taken of his sculpture, he sometimes transformed the photograph into a unique work of art, by adding corrections that would not be transcribed onto the marble, bronze or even the plaster. On rarer occasions, some photo sessions prompted a surprisingly poetic artistic input.

The 1,250 pictures taken by Eugène Druet, following Rodin instructions, were the fruit of an extraordinary collaboration that inspired the photographer's quasi-visionary approach to his employer's sculpture. Jacques-Ernest Bulloz and Adolphe Braun's approach was more business-minded. Their objective was to ensure the artist's works reached a broader public. After 1900, Rodin, then at the peak of his career, encouraged a group of Pictorialist photographers to begin taking pictures of his works. Mostly British or American, Stephen Haweis and Henry Coles, Edward Steichen, Gertrude Käsebier and Alvin Langdon Coburn photographed Rodin's sculptures.

By 1896, Rodin had incorporated photography into his creative oeuvre, and he began exhibiting prints beside his sculptures. The Pavillon de l'Alma exhibition in 1900 included 71 photographs. From then on, this was a usual feature of most of the exhibitions in which the sculptor took part. S. E.

140

GAUDENZIO MARCONI
(1842–1885)

Auguste Neyt, Model for "The Age of Bronze"

1877

Albumen print
H. 24 cm; W. 14.8 cm
Ph. 270

"I have unbounded admiration for the nude. I worship it," Rodin used to say. He sought out models with strong, vigorous bodies, whether they were professional or not. Auguste Neyt, a muscular telegraphist, who remained friends with the sculptor after posing for *The Age of Bronze* (6), was an amateur. At the time, Rodin was struggling to be recognized as an artist in his own right and was working relentlessly to produce a great piece of sculpture. Shown at the Salon des Artistes Belges, in Brussels, in 1877, the statue met with unanimous acclaim, although one art critic suspected Rodin of having used a life cast to make it. To quash this accusation, a few months later, Rodin turned for help to Gaudenzio Marconi, a prolific photographer of nudes. Intending to present the work again, this time at the Salon des Artistes Français, Paris, he commissioned Marconi to take photographs, from the front and back, of August Neyt naked, in the pose of *The Age of Bronze* (6). These efforts were, however, all in vain. The jury never even looked at the photographs.

S. E.

141

VICTOR PANNELIER
(1840 –AFTER 1907)

Clay Model of Eustache de Saint Pierre

Circa 1886

Studio at 117, boulevard de Vaugirard
Retouched in pen and black ink;
annotated in graphite pencil: *plein*
Albumen print
H. 37.7 cm; W. 16.7 cm
Ph. 317

When working on *The Burghers of Calais* (20-25), Rodin, in true academic style, made nude models of his figures first, to study the muscle structure, before cladding them in their famous tunics, as can be seen in several photographs by Charles Bodmer. But when he began to clothe his heroes, including the present figure of *Eustache de Saint Pierre*, he called upon the services of Victor Pannelier, who produced a genuine illustrated report. The additions to the robe in pen and ink made by Rodin show how the sculptor wanted to emphasize the contrasting light and shade effects, thus indicating how this photograph should be reproduced when used as an illustration.

As when photographing *Jean d'Aire* and *Andrieu d'Andres*, Pannelier opted for an oblong format, which he adapted so that only the figure was visible. Nevertheless, the image abounds in details of Rodin's working environment. Take, for example, the reproduction of Raphael's fresco, *Dispute of the Sacrament*, pinned onto the studio wall.

In 1899, the engraver Auguste Léveillé would use this photograph again as the model for a print in Léon Maillard's book *Auguste Rodin statuaire* and an issue of *La Revue Illustrée*, since it was impossible to publish a photograph directly. Many of the details were lost in the print. Neither the medium of the work nor the studio surroundings were recognizable and, as a result, the sculpture seems to be standing in a museum environment, totally out of context with its elaboration.

S. E.

142

EUGÈNE DRUET (1867-1916)
AND RODIN

Young Girl embraced by a Marble Ghost

Gelatin-silver print, with pencil highlights
H. 26 cm; W. 20 cm
PH 348

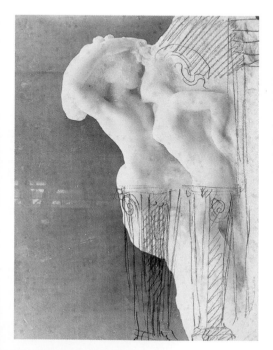

I n the words of Hélène Pinet, "Photography enabled Rodin to stand back and consider his work and he made good use of it. Judging a sculpture from a distance led him to make some amendments, or *pentimenti*, on the photographic reproductions of his sculptures," (Pinet, 2007).

Using a pencil to retouch the photo taken by Eugène Druet of the marble *Young Girl embraced by a Marble Ghost*, Rodin once again happily reinterpreted his own works, as he had done with his paper assemblages or in the reworked versions of his earlier drawings. Here, he placed the marble group upright, instead of leaving it in its usual horizontal position, and stood each of the two figures, from the hips down, on a moulded pedestal, thus transforming the ghost and the young woman into caryatids.

N. L.

143

ANONYMOUS

Birth of Venus emerging from the Waves

Circa 1889

Outlined in gouache, retouched
in graphite pencil; annotated in pen
and brown ink on the right:
Naissance de Vénus sortant de l'onde
Albumen print
H. 10 cm; W. 14,2 cm
Ph. 1053

Rodin had no qualms about tampering with photographs and thus added drawings or amendments in graphite pencil and gouache to this assemblage called *Birth of Venus emerging from the Waves*. These amendments went beyond a simple indication to modify a detail or improve a form. They became an autonomous drawing superimposed on the photographic image. The mechanical medium of photography and the manual medium of drawing fused into a singular work of art in its own right. These hybrid works were perhaps the reaction of a man attached to the idea of artistic creation, at a time when it was being increasingly aided by machines, especially in the field of decorative arts. Rodin thus appropriated photography. He incorporated its cold precision into his world by transforming it into a creative medium of his own.

S. E.

144

D. (OR E.) FREULER
(ACTIVE IN THE 1880S–AFTER 1909)

Marble Thought covered by a Cloth

Circa 1895

Salt print
H. 24.2 cm ; L. 17.6 cm
Ph. 1305

When Camille Claudel joined his studio, Rodin made several portraits and masks of her. In 1886-89, he modelled *Thought*, an allegorical work showing the face of the young woman, wearing a little pleated bonnet, emerging from a block of rough-hewn marble. In 1895, Rodin became interested in the effect of adding drapery to an earlier work (see *Draped Torso of The Age of Bronze*, **46**), or, as seen here, in the way in which a simple piece of fabric, placed over *Thought*, altered the appearance of a sculpture. Camille Claudel's face is veiled and in the shadow. Freuler captured and recorded the sculptor's spontaneous gesture in this photograph, thus turning it into an ephemeral variation of the work.

S. E

145

POL MARSAN DORNAC (?-1941)

Rodin in front of the "Monument to Sarmiento", Hands in Pockets, Tools placed on a Plank of Wood

1898

Studio at the Dépôt des Marbres – "Our Contemporaries at Home" series
Albumen print
H. 12.5 cm; W. 18 cm
Ph. 185

This portrait of Rodin belongs to a series entitled "Our Contemporaries at Home", featuring celebrities from the world of art and politics in the late 19th and early 20th century, published in the periodical *L'Art et les artistes*. The photographer, Pol Marsan Dornac, took pictures of his subjects with the tools of their trade, which made it easy to identify each person's occupation: Gustave Geffroy posed behind his desk, Verlaine sat in a café with a sheet of paper and a pen, the sculptor Rodin stood in front of a marble, surrounded by points, chisels and a hammer. In addition to the typological aspect of this series of portraits, Dornac demonstrated his skill in releasing the shutter at a magical moment. Rodin's presence has a rare intensity. In 1905, Rilke would describe the artist's aura in the following terms: "He then takes on a concentrated gaze that comes and goes like the beam cast by a light house, but with such a force that, even when far behind one, one can still feel its fury swelling."   S. E.

146

EUGÈNE DRUET (1867-1916)

The Kiss

Circa 1898

Studio at the Dépôt des Marbres
On the *verso*, in stencil and gouache:
A. Rodin, photographie, cadre n°354
Gelatin-silver print
H. 39.3 cm; W. 30 cm
Ph. 373

By 1896, Rodin was no longer content to work solely with photographers such as Pannelier, Charles Bodmer and Freuler, whose approach to taking pictures of works of art was purely technical. Probably tired of not being able to exercise any control over the way his works were photographed, and aware of Eugène Druet's talent, he made him his official photographer, a position he filled until 1903. Druet, an amateur photographer, was the owner of the French Yacht Club Café where Rodin usually ate, but he turned professional after meeting the sculptor, and went on to open his own art gallery and photo agency, in Rue Royale. This "photography buff" was clearly more open to the maestro's ideas than other photographers of the day. Rodin, who had decided to participate in the genesis of the photographs of his works, asked Druet to present *The Kiss* (**33**) in its natural environment, the studio. He himself signed this coproduction by adding the final touch – the mallet at the foot of the sculpture. In Rodin's view, the work was thus complete.

S. E.

147

EUGÈNE DRUET (1867-1916)

The Age of Bronze

Circa 1898

Dining-room at the Villa des Brillants,
Meudon
Gelatin-silver print
H. 39.6 cm; W. 29.9 cm
Ph. 1875

Serendipity can sometimes play a major role in artistic creation. Such was the case in this photograph of *The Age of Bronze* (6), taken by Eugène Druet in 1898. One day, the photographer came across an effect now known as "solarization". If a chlorobromide paper is exposed to the light while it is being developed in the darkroom (which may happen when the door is inadvertently opened), parts of the image will come out negative. As a result of this effect, *The Age of Bronze* (6) seems to be weightless here. Druet, encouraged by Rodin, adopted and attempted to master the process by producing a dozen or so variations, each one with a different degree of solarization. In the 20th century, solarization would be used as a technique and a means of photographic expression by artists such as Man Ray and Maurice Tabard.

S. E.

148

EDWARD STEICHEN
(1879–1973)

The Awakening

1902

Platinotype
H. 25 cm; W. 20 cm
Ph. 684

*T*he *Awakening*, also called the *Nymph Echo*, is known to exist in plaster versions, now in the Musée Rodin, and a marble dating from 1902, whose whereabouts today are uncertain. Inspired by Ovid's *Metamorphoses*, the sculpture represents a young woman, seated on a rock, stretching voluptuously.

Edward Steichen photographed *The Awakening* twice, from an almost identical angle, but playing on very different lighting effects. The first shot presents the work in a uniform light, with all the details of the sculpture clearly visible. The second photograph, shown here, is an against-the-light view of *The Awakening*. A piece of fabric attempts to soften the light coming through the studio window, but it is so bright that it transforms the sculpture into a silhouette and all the details have vanished. In what seems to be the early morning light, the effects suggested by the title of the work are heightened, rather like a metaphorical illustration. One may therefore suppose that Steichen only handled the first photograph in a conventional manner so that he might attempt a bolder – and fundamentally more pertinent – interpretation of *The Awakening*.

S. E.

In 1901, Steichen's dream came true when he was allowed to make several portraits of Rodin in his studio. He would have liked to photograph the sculptor posing beside two of his major works, *Monument to Victor Hugo* (39-40) and *The Thinker* (68), all on the same plate. But lack of space made this impossible. The following year, he therefore showed Rodin a photomontage composed of two different images. The sculptor was very impressed by the result: a profile view of him opposite *The Thinker* (68) and *Victor Hugo* (39). He laughed at his biographer Judith Clavel's turn of phrase, "Rodin, between God and the devil".

The photograph was published twice in 1905-06, in the periodical *Camera Work*, mouthpiece of the American Pictorialist photography movement. The concept behind the picture was highly innovative for the period in which it was taken, since it defied the idea of "realistic illusion", based on the veracity and accuracy of the content, the underlying canon of 19th-century photography. The Pictorialist image here no longer resembled a conventional photograph and this appealed to Rodin, for montages and assemblages were part of his own working method: "I sketch an arm, a leg, the head. And I stop there... Little by little, the body to which that leg, that arm, that head could be adapted outlines itself in my mind." (Rodin, 1910).

S. E.

149

EDWARD STEICHEN (1879-1973)

Rodin, the "Monument to Victor Hugo" and "The Thinker"

1902

Signed: STEICHEN / MDCCCCII
Bichromated-gelatin print
H. 26 cm ; W. 32.2 cm
Ph. 217

150

EDWARD STEICHEN (1879–1973)

Mask of Hanako

Platinotype
H. 24 cm; W. 20 cm
Ph. 673

In 1907, a turning-point in the history of photography, Steichen's friend, Alfred Stieglitz, took a picture entitled *The Steerage*, an image that marked the transition from Pictorialism to "pure photography", a movement that, unlike its predecessor, condemned any sort of image manipulation. This evolution could also be seen in Steichen's work after his famous series on the *Monument to Balzac* (**158**), dating from 1908, in the shots of *Hanako*, taken between 1911 and 1913. The choice of a more difficult, more fragile subject is striking. There is no question here of imitating painterly effects. Everything comes into play at the moment the picture is taken, using the medium's own means: light, focusing, depth of field, perspective, angle. From then on, Steichen no longer explored image-altering effects. He printed his photographs with what Europeans considered a particularly soft use of contrast, on platinotype paper, since this process had the advantage of producing a wide range of greys from the negative plate. While Pictorialism had enabled photography to free itself from its "scientific tool" label and join the other artistic disciplines, this movement did not outlive the revolution it had brought about. Photography's emancipation and acceptance as an art form in its own right would stem from the recognition of its individual, reality-bound aesthetic.

S. E.

151

STEPHEN HAWEIS & HENRY COLES
(1878-1969 / 1875-?)

Pierre de Wissant,

1903-1904

Bichromated-gelatin print (?)
H. 21.5 cm; W. 17 cm
Ph. 960

To obtain the disquieting atmosphere found in some of their photographs, Haweis and Coles used artificial lighting, acetylene gas lamps, for example. This kind of lighting gave rise to strong contrast, reinforced by the rich blacks of the bichromated-gelatin print. Henry Coles, who printed this photograph, deliberately exaggerated the shadows formed by the folds of the fabric, which thus contributed to the dramatic effect of the *mise-en-scène*.

This shot of *Pierre de Wissant* suggests the new aesthetic inspired by Symbolism that would develop shortly after Rodin's death: Expressionist cinema.

S. E.

152

STEPHEN HAWEIS & HENRY COLES
(1878-1969 / 1875-?)

Crouching Woman

1903-1904
Carbon print
H. 22.1 cm; W. 17 cm
Ph. 297

Not counting Druet, Haweis and Coles were the first of Rodin's photographers to experiment with artificial light. Now associated with the Pictorialist movement, the two British artists – Haweis was a painter – took about 200 photographs for Rodin in under two years. "We shall come... and show you half a dozen photographs of Mr Kelly's bronze *Crouching Woman* taken in artificial light, which I think are very good." While they no doubt intially chose this type of lighting so as to be able to take photographs inside, it soon helped them to develop an innovative aesthetic approach.

This against-the-light shot of *Crouching Woman* (71-72) shows a less provocative figure than the sculpture with which we are familar: her outspread knees are still visible, but her genitalia are hidden in the shadow and the emphasis, here, is on her facial expression.

S. E.

In 1903, Rodin ended his collaboration with his appointed photographer, Eugène Druet, who was about to open an art gallery. The sculptor began looking for a professional photographer who could cope with the growing demand for reproductions of his work. The photography publisher Jacques-Ernest Bulloz met all his requirements: a good technician and rigorous manager, he signed an exclusive contract with Rodin on 5 May 1903, which lasted until the artist's death 15 years later. Bulloz not only worked as a photographer for the sculptor, but also gradually took charge of all the paperwork concerning the distribution of photographs of Rodin's oeuvre, even those taken by other photographers, such as Haweis and Coles. The work portrayed here, *Head of Sorrow*, which first appeared circa 1882 in *The Gates of Hell* (11-14), appeared recurrently in Rodin's oeuvre. It was enlarged after 1900, and the present marble version was photographed by Bulloz, who always took pictures of Rodin's works for commercial and documentary purposes. The faithful reproduction of the object to be represented governed his technical and aesthetic approach. He worked methodically and laid the foundations of photographic conventions related to museum exhibits that are still observed today. The subject is isolated through the use of a backdrop. While the depth of field covers the sculpture, the background remains deliberately hazy, to make the subject stand out. Bulloz worked with both a principal and a secondary source of light. Whenever there was only one source of light available, a studio window, for example, he created a second one with the help of a reflector. He thus succeeded in conveying to perfection the volumes of a sculpture, to which he then added fabulous shades of colour by using a photographic process called carbon printing.

S. E.

153

JACQUES-ERNEST BULLOZ
(1858-1942)

Head of Sorrow

1903-1904

Carbon print
H. 33.3 cm; W. 26 cm
Ph. 978

154

JEAN LIMET (1855-1941)

Monument to the Burghers of Calais

Circa 1904

Bichromated-gelatin print
H. 28.5 cm; W. 39.1 cm
Ph. 7006

In 1895, the Monument to the *Burghers of Calais* (20-25) was unveiled in their home city. Circa 1904, the sculptor asked Jean Limet, a painter by trade who had become the appointed patinator of his bronzes, to photograph the group: "very low, to let the public penetrate the heart of the subject, as in church entombments, where the group is almost on ground level." Limet photographed the *Burghers* from behind, to create the illusion of a procession, in keeping with the contemporary trend away from realistic photography towards an Impressionistic vision. The new theories of the Pictorialist school defended personal interpretation and participation. From then on, the photographer was regarded as an artist in his own right. The graininess of the bichromated-gelatin print and the radiographic effects that Limet obtained enabled him to dematerialize the contours and introduce colour into the sculpture. To tone his photographs, he used almost the same products as those he employed for his patinas. He thus obtained multiple variations in tone that contribute to the impact of these photographs of the *Burghers* walking to their death like an army of ghosts.

S. E.

155

JACQUES-ERNEST BULLOZ
(1858-1942)

General View
of the Studio in Meudon

1904-1905

Gelatin-silver print
H. 27.5 cm; W. 37 cm
Ph. 966

To coincide with the 1900 Exposition Universelle, Rodin organized an independent exhibition of his works in the Pavillon de l'Alma, a temporary venue halfway between a gallery and a studio. On view inside were a large number of sculptures, mostly plasters, often studies or fragments, as well as photographs and drawings. Funded by the bankers Dorizon, Albert Kahn and Joanny Peytel, the Pavillon de l'Alma was built by Alexandre Marcel and Louis Sortais. The sculptor had given a great deal of thought to its architecture and lighting. Although he would have liked to leave it standing on the Parisian site, it was taken down when the exhibition closed and rebuilt in his garden at Meudon, in 1901. It retained its gallery-cum-studio function and housed the works that Rodin showed people who came to see him in Meudon. The photographer Jacques-Ernest Bulloz took this shot from above, perched on the steps of the studio staircase. He used a wide-angle lens to garner a maximum of information in one image. This panoramic view provides an idea of what visitors to this fascinating place in Rodin's day must have found: a forest of white plaster statues, bathed in dazzling light.

S. E.

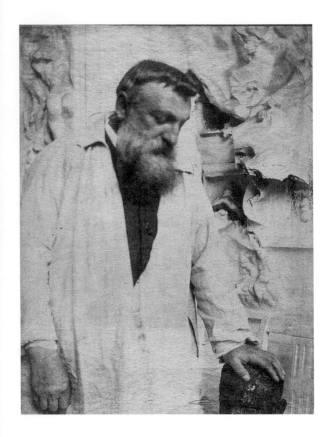

156

GERTRUDE KÄSEBIER (1852-1934)

Rodin in front of "The Gates of Hell", with Left Hand resting on the Bronze Head of Baron d'Estournelles de Constant

1905

Bichromated-gelatin print
H. 33 cm; W. 25 cm
Ph. 249

At the height of his career, Rodin occasionally exchanged one of his sculptures or drawings for a photograph, as he did, in 1913, for this portrait by Gertrude Käsebier.

Close to Alfred Stieglitz and a member of the Linked Ring group, she came to Paris in 1905 to photograph Rodin. She brought her own special universe with her: her allegorical images handled subjects such as mother-daughter relationships, families and old age. While her version of the sculptor as a creative genius is thus close to the works of her fellow Pictorialists, one by no means insignificant detail makes her vision unique: she was the only woman to have ever photographed Rodin.

S. E.

157

ALVIN LANGDON COBURN
(1882–1966)

George Bernard Shaw in the Pose of "The Thinker"

April 1906

Inscribed in pencil, lower right:
To M. Auguste Rodin from Alvin Langdon Coburn September 15th 1906
Carbon on platinotype
H. 29.2 cm; W. 23 cm
Ph. 1214

George Bernard Shaw opened numerous doors for the young photographer Alvin Langdon Coburn, when he arrived in England in 1904 with the ambitious idea of making photographic portraits of all the celebrities of the day. Shaw introduced Coburn to Rodin, whom he knew well, having posed for a bust modelled by the sculptor. In 1906, the photographer and the writer attended the unveiling of *The Thinker* **(68)**. On the way home, Shaw suggested that Coburn make a nude portrait of him, in the same pose as the sculpture, thereby launching a genre that would become popular in the 20th century. Joining a gallery of hundreds of conventional photographic portraits – which always showed a face emerging from a garment – was, in fact, an idea he found extremely tedious. Coburn thought it was a narcissistic suggestion, but produced this provocative portrait. "I beg you to accept a photograph I am sending you that I call *The Thinker*," he wrote in a letter accompanying a print addressed to Rodin. When the infamous portrait, which nobody had seen while Shaw was alive, was first published, several journalists asked for confirmation of the model's name.

S. E.

158

EDWARD STEICHEN (1879-1973)

The Open Sky, 11 p.m.

1908

On the *verso*, in graphite pencil: *grey blue*
Carbon print
H. 25.2 cm; W. 22 cm
Ph. 235

"Your photographs will make the world understand my Balzac," Rodin said eagerly in 1908, when Edward Steichen showed him the nocturnal *Balzac* series. Rodin had not forgotten the scandal that broke out in 1898 over the work he considered the very essence of his aesthetic (50-52, 65). Rodin's statue had made a big impression on the young Pictorialist photographer, when he was still living in the United States and when a local newspaper, based in Milwaukee (Wisconsin), had published a picture of the work. Seven years after the two men first met in Paris, the sculptor commissioned Steichen to photograph his *Balzac* – still only in its plaster state – "by moonlight".

Steichen spent two entire nights working in the gardens in Meudon, exploring all the possibilities of taking pictures by moonlight – a new experience – and, using very long exposure times lasting from 30 minutes to two hours, produced some spectacular shots. He carefully noted down the time at which he took each picture – *The Open Sky* was taken at 11pm – and where he stood. He was such a perfectionist that he then spent several weeks in his laboratory to find the unique greenish blue tint that enhances the night effect. He himself wrote that his photograph looked so much like a canvas that he felt he had "painted" *Balzac*.

S. E.

Commissioned in 1889, the *Monument to Victor Hugo* (39-40) portrays the poet seated in a contemplative pose. It should have been erected outside the Panthéon, but since its composition was judged to be too confused, the local authorities found it a home in the gardens of the Palais Royal. Documentary evidence of trial installations of monuments on a site is rare. These pictures of a provisional plaster model, taken by F. Bianchi at Rodin's request, are therefore all the more valuable. Bianchi shows us the various stages leading up to the final installation of the marble. This illustrated report highlights the importance of the setting – the very graphic silhouette of the bare tree, the emphatic black lines of its branches. One of the photographs gave rise to the metaphor coined by the press of a boat lying high and dry, whereas Rodin saw "tormented branches buffeted by the sea wind".

S. E.

159

F. BIANCHI (ACTIVE IN PARIS IN THE EARLY 20TH CENTURY)

Monument to Victor Hugo, Trial Installation, in the Gardens of the Palais Royal, Paris

March 1909

Matt collodion aristotype print
H. 17.5 cm; 23.5 cm
Ph. 1114

Bénédicte GARNIER

Antiques

I n the early 1890s, when living in Meudon, Rodin began to collect ancient works of art from Egypt, Greece and Rome, then later from the Far East. Fragments of Venuses, Greek vases and Egyptian figurines in bronze invaded the spaces in which he worked and lived, replacing the rare casts after Antique statues, traditionally present in a sculptor's studio. As Rodin's fame grew, the many commissions he received enabled him to purchase over 6,000 works of art between 1893 and 1917.

The influence of the Antique was hardly foreign to Rodin, trained in his youth, like all 19th-century artists, to copy Greco-Roman models in the Louvre or from albums of engravings in the Bibliothèque Impériale. But his interest revived in the 1890s, like a source of rejuvenation, nurtured by his past experience and fully internalized. It was no longer a question of copying, but of living and creating in the manner of the ancient masters, in adoration of Nature. The sculptor regarded his collection of antiques as being crucial to his own creative output. He purchased countless fragments of Greek and Roman marbles from antiquarians such as Élie Géladakis and Spiridon Castellanos. Rodin searched for Antique statues in the incomplete state in which they had come down through the ages to measure his own fragmentary sculptures, *Meditation* (48) or *The Walking Man* (73), for example, against them. He also bought Greek vases and a vast selection of ceramics. From this abundant repertory of forms, he drew new inspiration for his sculpture which he then incorporated into his assemblages (59, 60). The archaeological find thus changed status and became part of his oeuvre.

From 1910-12 onwards, Rodin was already thinking about assembling his works, collections and archives in a future museum. Encouraged by the antiquarian Joseph Altounian, who was based in Cairo, he completed his Egyptian collection. In 1916, the collection of Antiques was part of the donation that Rodin made to the French state, which founded the Musée Rodin.   B. G.

ANONYMOUS
The collection of Antiques beneath the peristyle of the Pavillon de l'Alma, Meudon,
1906-1917
Ph. 2709

160

EGYPTIAN ART

Fragment of a False-Door Stele

Old Kingdom, 5th-4th Dynasty (circa 2500-2170 BC)

Limestone
H. 35 cm; W. 72 cm; D. 9.8 cm
Acquired by Rodin
between 1893 and 1913
Co. 1301

In the days of the Old Kingdom, the false-door stele – a reproduction of the door to an Egyptian house – in a private tomb symbolized the passage between the earthly world and the afterlife. Offerings were placed in front of it. In the central panel here, the seated figure of the deceased is carved in bas-relief, wearing a long striated wig, her hand stretched towards a small table laden with bread. The woman is about to eat a meal forever engraved in stone. Above her and on the lintel, lines of hieroglyphs list the offerings of meat, incense, cosmetics and vases. The delicately carved bas-relief has lost all of its painted decoration. The use of the canon of proportion within an 18-square grid confers a geometric appearance on the female figure and limits the angle from which her body is seen to profile and front views.

B. G.

161

<small>EGYPTIAN ART</small>

Fragment of a Sunken Relief: Wall from the Tomb of Pay

18th Dynasty (circa 1539-1292 BC)

Limestone
H. 35.5 cm; W. 88 cm; D. 5.5 cm
Acquired by Rodin
between 1893 and 1913
Co. 1302

This relief comes from the tomb built by Pay, overseer of the royal harem, during the reign of Tutankhamun (1333-23 BC), later completed by his son and successor, Raia, at Saqqara, the vast necropolis situated in the Memphis region. It was probably placed on the south wall of the tomb's inner courtyard. Depicted on the relief is a series of scenes in which priests, clad in long pleated loincloths and shoulder-length wigs with curled locks, pour libations in front of wooden pavilions, where offerings of food and flowers are piled up. Inscribed above each scene is a lament citing the name of Pay. The relief obtained by carving the contours and subjects deep into the stone, catches the light more keenly than bas-relief, thereby accentuating the narrative precision and stylistic preciosity.

B. G.

162

Egyptian art

Head of a Man

Late Period, 25th-27th Dynasty (715-404 BC)

Limestone
H. 22 cm; W. 10.8 cm; D. 19 cm
Acquired by Rodin
between 1893 and 1917
Co. 3078

This head belonged to a statue of a man with dorsal pillar, the beginning of which is still visible at the back. The subject is represented without a wig. His close-cropped hair, shown in slight relief, is indicated by a single line which outlines and enhances his facial features. The Egyptian sculptor skilfully rendered the juvenile grace of this young man, his almond-shaped eyes and the lines of expression around his smiling mouth. Without indulging in the art of the portrait, he rejected the idealized expression of eternal youth, dear to the artists of previous centuries, in order to depict a type of age and character more realistically.

B. G.

163

EGYPTIAN ART

Statue of King Ptolemy III Euergetes I

Ptolemaic Period (332–30 BC)

Limestone
H. 85 cm; W. 32.3 cm; D. 39.1 cm
Acquired by Rodin from the antiquarian
Joseph Altounian in August 1912
Co. 1414

This now fragmentary royal statue with a dorsal pillar was dedicated to the cult of King Ptolemy III Euergetes I, the "Benefactor", the third sovereign of the Ptolemaic dynasty from Macedonia, who ruled over Egypt from 246 BC to 221 BC. The figure, represented in the act of walking, wears a loincloth, or schenti, held up by a belt. On his upper chest, there are traces of a pendant that may have been adorned with an image of the goddess Maat. The three columns of hieroglyphs on the dorsal pillar sing the king's praises. The work was chosen by Joseph Altounian in 1912. The quality of this block of compact stone, enlivened by the effects of light and shadow on the loincloth and dorsal pillar, no doubt appealed to Rodin who was so fond of the "hieratic quality" of Egyptian art and the "geometric austerity of nature" (Rodin in Canudo, 1913).

B. G.

164

ASSYRIAN ART

Fragment of a Bas-Relief: Head of a Median Tribute-Bearer

732-705 BC

Gypseous alabaster
H. 23.5 cm; W. 18 cm; D. 7.9 cm
Acquired by Rodin on 4 March 1908
from the antiquarian Spiridon Castellanos.
Co. 6401

This relief comes from the decorative frieze in a corridor leading to the main courtyard of the Assyrian King Sargon II's palace in Khorsabad (present-day Iraq), discovered in 1843. The head belongs to the scene showing a procession of tribute-bearers from all the surrounding countries, bringing offerings to the king in sign of their submission. It is a portrait of a tribute-bearer from Media, an area northwest of Iran, recognizable from his beard and short hair carved in concentric circles, held down by a headband. Rodin purchased this head described as "savage, withdrawn, locked in a dream of conquest and carnage" in 1908. The sculptor admired the sensuality and warlike character of this art which he first saw in the early 1880s at the British Museum, London. He made sketches there of bearded men and lion's heads, which he then incorporated into his work on the *Bust of Victor Hugo*, in 1883 **(18)**.

B. G.

165

GREEK ART

Fragment
of a Funerary Stele

3rd quarter of the 4th century BC

Marble
H. 88 cm; W. 51.5 cm; D. 7.7 cm
Acquired by Rodin
between 1893 and 1913
Co. 493

In the Greek world, particularly in Athens, the funerary stele, erected on the tomb of the deceased, was decorated with a carved relief. Here, the deceased is represented seated on a stool, clad in a tunic and cloak, and surrounded by her family. The loss of part of the relief has cropped the composition. Standing behind the main figure, one can still identify a man leaning on a walking stick, in front of the head of a servant, whose hand is pressed to her face in sign of mourning. Traces of a child's hand can be seen on the knees of the deceased. Owing to the fragmentation of the scene, the focus now falls on the deceased, who stands out in high relief and, according to Rodin, assumes her full value in space. The fragments of the other figures, tapering upwards in weaker relief and offering relatively legible evidence of what has been lost, are now accidentally assembled in a new composition with the face and drapery of the deceased.

B. G.

166

GREEK ART

Weeping Siren

2nd half of the 4th century BC

Marble with traces of red-ochre
and blue-green polychromy
H. 39.5 cm; W. 25 cm; D. 13 cm
Acquired by Rodin
between 1893 and 1903
Co. 412

This figure of a siren with outspread wings once
adorned an acroterion, the decorative motif at the
apex of a funerary stele. This sea monster, with a woman's
head and bust on a bird's body and feet, conventionally
beat her breast while her mournful singing accompanied
the funeral cortege. In 1903, this statue could be admired
on Rodin's dining-room table, in the Villa des Brillants,
Meudon. Rodin ignored the traces of ancient polychromy to concentrate on the play of light and shadow
that enlivened the modelling of the statue, coloured pale
amber by the earth from which it was excavated. The
sculptor liked its simplified form that mirrored his own
sketches of vase-like women with hour-glass bodies,
enhanced by ochre water-colours, whose arm movements sometimes resembled the handle of an amphora
(109). Her tilted head, dreamy expression and melan-
choly wailing prompt us to re-examine the countless
female figures on *The Gates of Hell* **(11-14)**, including the
Three Sirens group that made its appearance before 1887

B. G.

167

Greek art

Attic Red-Figure Column-Krater

Circa 470 BC

Terracotta
H. 43 cm; Diam. 35 cm
Acquired by Rodin
between 1893 and 1913
Co. 3153

A krater – from the Greek word for "mixing bowl" – was used in Antiquity to dilute wine with water at a secular banquet. Two handles, shaped like small columns, are placed either side of a wide mouth. On the front of the body, a man playing a lyre holds out a cup to a dancing figure. On the back, an ephebe carries an oenochoe, a Greek jug with a single handle, which was dipped into the krater to be filled before serving the wine. In "red-figure" decorations, the painter drew the outlines of the motif on the vase after it had been dried by the potter. The figures and patterns were left unglazed, and thus retained the colour of the clay, while the rest was covered in a shiny black glaze, which was also used to add fine detail to the drapery, musculature and faces. The vase was then fired to complete the process. The decoration of this vase is attributed to an artist known as the "Pig Painter".

B. G.

168

GREEK ART

Attic Red-Figure Kalyx Krater

mid-4th century BC

Terracotta
H. 31.5 cm; Diam. 26 cm
Acquired by Rodin
between 1893 and 1913
Co. 215

This deep-bowled vase has a very elongated neck, opening outwards into a wide-mouthed chalice, which enables the figures to be depicted over the full height of the vase. The main scene represents Eros, the god of love, flying in front of two ephebes, standing either side of an ithyphallic Herm. On the other side are three draped ephebes. The vase was made in the workshop of an Attic potter in the mid-4th century. The red-figure decoration is attributed to an artist known as "Rodin's Painter". He used Kertch-style white highlights to emphasize the importance of the Herm and play up the characteristic attributes of each figure.

B. G.

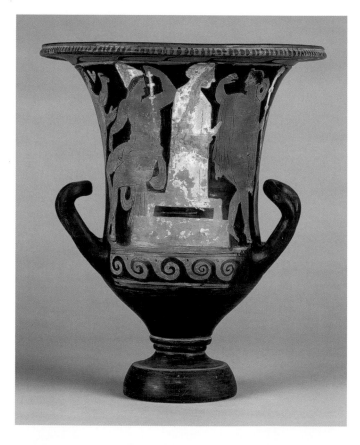

169

<small>ETRUSCAN ART</small>

Ephebe

3rd–2nd century BC

Bronze
H. 24.8 cm; W. 8.5 cm; D. 3.5 cm
Acquired by Rodin
between 1893 and 1917
Co. 1329

This male statuette from pre-Roman Italy stirs the imagination with its raw, primitive appearance, its facial features barely indicated by pinchmarks in the original clay. Rodin liked the sombre side of Etruscan artists and the dryness of the bronze sculptures eaten away by oxidization. The monumentality of this modest-sized work recalls Rodin's own investigations, into the figure of *Walking Man* (**73**), for example, "I have always sought the architectural aspect of the human body... The work is present in each of the planes... Forms repeat themselves in nature. But there is something that remains: the form. The Ancients always understood that, and they sought the "core" of each form, the very essence of its appearance, caring little for details of the object that they actually had before their eyes." (Rodin in Canudo, 1913).

B. G.

170

ROMAN ART

Kore

Ist century BC

Marble
H. 78 cm; W. 34 cm; D. 21.8 cm
Acquired by Rodin
between 1893 and 1913
Co. 271

This is a statue of a standing woman, clad in the tunic and cloak typical of Ionian statues of young women dating from the late 6th or early 5th century BC. This Roman copy pleased Rodin's taste for Archaic sculpture, also illustrated in the collection by the casts of the *Hera of Samos* and *Apollo of Thera*. Here, he again found simplified forms and graphic drapery creating geometric planes and effects of light and shadow. Rodin liked to group the different arts of the past together in aesthetic families. Medieval art, of which he constantly made drawings, was placed beyond the barriers of time, alongside Archaic Greek art: "The pleated drapery [found in] this cathedral is the sort of pleated drapery Archaic Greece always loved; it enables one to fill spaces with sharp lines and to respect planes by adorning them." (Rodin in Judrin, 1992).

B. G.

171

ROMAN ART

Seated Venus,
known as *Agrippina*

2nd century AD

Marble
H. 93 cm; W. 118 cm; D. 48 cm
Acquired by Rodin from the antiquarian
Gaston Neumans on 9 April 1909
Co. 471

Wearing a long tunic and a cloak, the woman here is represented seated on a high-backed chair. A similar statue in the Capitoline Museum, Rome, was given the name Agrippina in the 17th century. The work is also known as *Seated Aphrodite*, the title of the original Greek statue carved by Phidias, in the 5th century BC. Replicas of this statue made in the Roman period were used as honorary or funerary portraits of women. Rodin purchased the statue in 1909 and exhibited it under the peristyle of the Pavillon de l'Alma, in Meudon, as an introduction to his own plaster sculptures. Nearby, to create a mirror effect, he placed his torso of *Cybele,* which had been enlarged in 1904, another partially seated, headless figure, with her only arm pointing to the ground. In the present figure, as on the ancient statue mutilated by time, Rodin refused to include any attribute that would help identify the woman. Only the mythological title of the work enables us to ascribe it to a tradition.

B. G.

172

ROMAN ART

Portrait of a Scholar: Thucydidus?

(460/455–400 BC), AD 69–96

Marble
H. 38.5 cm; W. 21 cm; D. 23 cm
Acquired by Rodin between 1893 and 1917
Co. 432

This Roman marble portrait is commonly associated with representations of Thucydidus, an Athenian historian and politician who lived in the 5th century BC. The sculptor captured the likeness of an ageing man, with a serious, pensive expression and heavily lined face, wreathed in the wavy curls of his beard and skilfully carved hair. In this portrait, Rodin could see "that critical period in life which the artist rendered in all its moving truthfulness" (Rodin, 1914). Even as a young man, Rodin had always compared his investigations, into the bust of *Man with the Broken Nose* (4), for example, with the ancient portraits in the Louvre. From 1895 onwards, his collection of Roman portraits juxtaposed his own countless projects for portraits, creating a veritable repertory of forms of expression.

B. G.

173

ROMAN ART

Portrait of Gaius Caesar?

20 BC–AD 4

Marble
H. 34.5 cm; W. 18.8 cm; D. 20.5 cm
Acquired by Rodin between 1893 and 1917
Co. 374

This Roman head probably came from a statue of Gaius Caesar (20 BC–AD 4) depicted in a toga. Son of Julia and Agrippa, he and his brother, Lucius, were adopted in 17 BC by their grandfather, Emperor Augustus, who wanted to make these two children his heirs. They received the titles of "Prince of Youth" and "Caesar", but died before they could reign.

This serene, juvenile portrait, made before Gaius' death, corresponds to Rodin's ideal of the Antique: a face composed of broad planes, with neither hollows nor holes, at times visible beneath the concretions and the earth in which it was buried. The sculptor abandoned himself to the contemplation of the Antique, loved its gentle sensuality, and said that he drew reassurance and encouragement to pursue his own work from it.

B. G.

174

HELLENISTIC OR ROMAN ART

Crouching Venus Anadyomene

Late Hellenistic or Early Imperial Period

Marble
H. 25 cm; W. 20 cm; D. 22 cm
Acquired by Rodin from the antiquarian
Spiridon Castellanos on 30 June 1910
Co. 562

175

ROMAN ART

Fragment of a Male Head

1st–2nd century AD(?)

Marble
H.16.3 cm; W. 9.5 cm; D. 14 cm
Acquired by Rodin from the antiquarian
Costis Lembessis in August 1904?
Co. 753

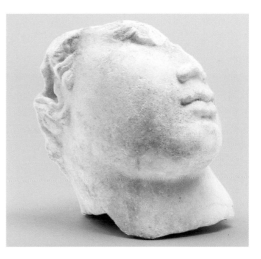

The figure of Venus is shown naked, here, having barely emerged from the waves. Only the crouching body has survived, leaving us to imagine the head of the goddess and the gesture of her arms lifting up her hair. The now fragmentary form seems to be turned in on itself, on an almost frontal plane, enlivened by the contradictory positions of the arms and legs.

Rodin purchased the statue in 1910 and exhibited it in 1912-13 in his museum at the Hôtel Biron. The sculptor had particular empathy for the crouching body theme, the very symbol of femininity and probably knew the Alexandrine origin of this antique: "Egyptian marble – It's a world in itself, an Egyptian Mona Lisa, a crouching Venus, as well as a living flower, a form whose powerful vigour and grace fill me with joy... This little fragment is a masterpiece," (Musée Rodin Archives, Rodin's notes).

B. G.

This anonymous fragment, broken diagonally, belongs to a Roman head of a man, copied from an original 5th-century Greek work, inspired by the sculptor Polycletes. Rodin loved the roundness of the cheek and the sensuality of the mouth, the lively expression that he attributed to Praxiteles' genius. He liked the evocative force of next to nothing in this fragment, purchased in August 1904. He exhibited it and had it photographed from every angle, on a plinth in his garden in Meudon. From it, he drew the daily encouragement he needed to persevere in his art: "This simple fragment has given my life direction, ensured my tranquillity and restored my desire. And happy to thus approach the Antique and admire it more on seeing it continually growing, I rediscover each day this same exquisite mouth and this divine equilibrium," (Rodin, 1904).

B. G.

176

Roman art

Colossal Left Hand holding Drapery

1st century AD

Marble
H. 21.2 cm; W. 23.5 cm; D. 29 cm
Gift to Rodin from John Marshall
on 2 January 1914
Co. 561

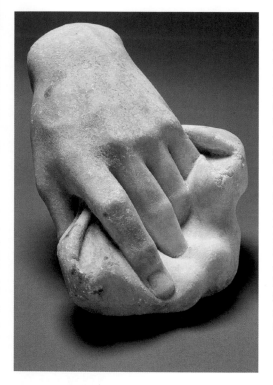

All that remains of a larger-than-life statue of a man is this broken left hand clutching a piece of drapery. Gentle and full of energy at the same time, it was carved with precision and the veins that are apparent infuse it with life. The archaeologist and art dealer John Marshall bought it in Rome and gave it to Rodin on 1 January 1914. The sculptor thanked him for this fragment, which, in his eyes, had the grandeur "of an antique or a Bernini" (Courtesy Ashmolean Library-University of Oxford). In Rodin's studio, fragments of antique hands, purchased in abundance, lay amongst the countless studies of hands modelled by the sculptor as independent works or separated from a statue in his experiments on fragmentation.

B. G.

177

SPANISH ART, CASTILLE

Virgin and Child

Circa 1300

Wood (Scots pine) with traces
of polychromy and early gilding
and parts repainted at a later date
H. 58 cm; W. 21.7 cm; D. 15.4 cm
Gift to Rodin from Igniacio Zuloaga
on 30 June 1914
Co. 3479

The Virgin is represented seated on a throne, holding the Christ Child on her left knee. She is clad in a cloak which falls open to reveal a loose dress and wears a veil and a royal crown. Her right hand holds the flower representing the Jesse Tree, the emblem of Christ's geneal-ogy, which also symbolizes the Immaculate Conception, the cult of which was widespread at this time. The Child, depicted bare-headed and clothed in a tunic, makes the sign of the benediction with his right hand, and holds a sphere, the symbol of eternity, in his left. This hieratic work, characteristic of early 14th-century Castilian style, was pur-chased in Spain for Rodin, in 1908, by the painter Ignacio Zuloaga, a great collector of medieval art. In 1905, the sculptor had discovered the masters of Iberian art in his com-pany, on a journey from Madrid to Seville via Toledo and Cordoba. Rodin did not receive the statue of the *Virgin and Child* until 1914.

B. G.

178

FRENCH ART, BOURGES

Mourner

Mid-15th century

Alabaster
H. 41 cm; W. 12.8 cm; D. 11.4 cm
Former collections of Mercier,
Romagnesi and Émile Molinier.
Acquired by Rodin on 3 January 1917
from the antiquarian Bacri in Paris
through the antiquarian Charles Mori,
from the former Fitzhenry Collection,
London?
Co. 914

This figure, clad in mourning clothes, holding a book, was placed in an alabaster recess in the base of the tomb of Jean de France, Duc de Berry (1340-1416) in the Sainte-Chapelle, Bourges. With 26 other mourners in various attitudes, he formed the funeral cortege of the deceased, represented as a gisant on the top of the tomb. In the early 15th century, Duc Jean de Berry had commissioned his sepulture from the sculptor Jean de Cambrai, who carved the recumbent figure and at least five of the mourners before 1438. The Musée Rodin's mourner was carved by a second team of sculptors, known as the "Flemish" artists, who were active in Bourges circa 1450. Purchased by Rodin in 1917, at the very end of his life, this image of mourning seems to complete his collection. It illustrates his interest in medieval art, which showed through in his research into the rendering of draped bodies or the expression of human distress, for example in the *Burghers of Calais* group **(20-25)**. B. G.

179

KATSUSHIKA HOKUSAI
(1760–1849)

The River Tama in the Province of Musashi

Circa 1832

Nishiki-e, polychrome woodcut
Ôban format, H. 25.9 cm; W. 37.7 cm
Gift to Rodin from the staff of the
Japanese review *Shirakaba* in July 1911
G. 7416

This print is the eighth view in the series called *Thirty-Six Views of Mount Fuji* by Hokusai. The landscape is cut in two by the band of mist that separates the mountain from the river. The extremely subtle use of blue intensifies the movement of the water and the expressivity of the scenery. The figures, one leading his horse and gazing at the mountain from the shore, the others crossing the river in a boat, add a touch of informality without perturbing the harmony and timeless calm of the landscape into which they merge. Rodin admired Hokusai's freedom of handling, the simplicity of his interpretation and the virtuosity of his colours. He saw a reflection of his own aspirations.

B. G.

Véronique MATTIUSSI, *Hélène* PINET

Archives

T he artist who is also a collector, archivist, curator and custodian of his own works has become a familiar figure over the last few years. Rodin was a perfect example. Probably through intuition rather than reflection, he knew how important the things that made up his daily universe would be to the understanding of his oeuvre. He thus kept everything. The tens of thousands of handwritten or printed documents, the books and periodicals that he donated to the French nation at the same time as his sculptures and collections, vividly recall more than 70 years of Rodin's private, social and artistic life. Thanks to these documents, we gain insight into the very heart of his creative process.

While the notes and rough drafts written in his hand shed light on his innermost thoughts, the letters he received open the doors to a much vaster world. They came from over 7,000 correspondents, including Rainer Maria Rilke, Octave Mirbeau, Ricciotto Canudo, Edward Steichen, Antoine Bourdelle, Poilane and Monsieur Pion. Research has shown that famous, not so famous and completely unknown names each tell the story of an episode in Rodin's life.

Cuttings from French and international newspapers, saved by Rodin, who subscribed to the Press Argus from 1883 onwards, enrich our investigations into his oeuvre. These thousands of articles mention the critics who spoke of his sculptures and the names of a huge network of friends and contacts that he built up over the years.

The sculptor's library constitutes the last piece of this vast puzzle. Books with dedications from the great writers or critics of the day (Rilke, Mirbeau, Gustave Geoffroy) stand alongside the reviews and works that Rodin consulted before tackling commissions such as the *Monument to Balzac* (52). Because Rodin donated everything to the French state in 1916, the coherence of his archives has remained intact. Their wealth and complexity continue to provide material for research on the world of art at the turn of the 20th century.

H. P.

180

Letter from Auguste Rodin to Rose Beuret (1844-1917)

Early 1876

Ink on paper
H. 21 cm; W. 13.8 cm
Inv. L.6

While still unknown to the public, Rodin realized a youthful dream by making an eagerly-planned visit to Italy, a compulsory step in any artistic career.

On his travels, he sent this unique document to his loyal companion, Rose Beuret, whom he did not marry until 1916, shortly before her death.

Among the artist's earliest manuscripts, this very moving letter describes the route he had followed before arriving in Rome and attests to the close rapport that the two young people had, while heralding his development as a sculptor.

Rose was the first of his many female assistants and here he urges her to take care of his works in his absence. Meanwhile, in Florence, the young sculptor came face to face with the great masters of the Italian Renaissance and studied Michelangelo and Donatello. In search of a formal vocabulary, Rodin was disconcerted, overwhelmed, by the works of Michelangelo that he discovered. The emotional quality of the modelling, the tormented poses and the muted force stemming from his unfinished works reassured Rodin, while revealing new paths for him to explore.

V. M.

« Te dire que je fais depuis la première heure que je suis à florence, une etude de Michel Ange ne t'etonnera pas, et je crois que ce grand magicien me laisse un peu de ses secrets. Cependant aucun de ses eleves, ni de ses maîtres, ne font comme lui Ce que je ne comprends pas, car je cherche dans ses éleves directs, mais ce n'est que dans lui, lui seul, où est le secret. j'ai fait des croquis le soir chez moi, non pas d'après ses œuvres mais d'après tous les echafaudages les systèmes que je fabrique dans mon imagination pour le comprendre, eh bien je réussi selon moi à leur donner l'allure ce quelque chose sans nom que lui seul sait donner. »

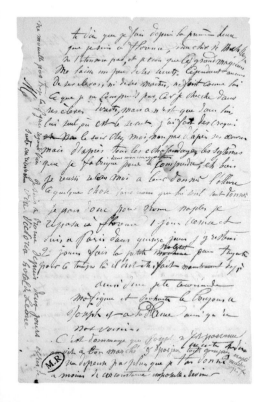

181

Letter from Octave Mirbeau (1848-1917) to Auguste Rodin

Early September 1885

Ink on paper
H. 17.5 cm; W. 11.4 cm
Ms. 775

"Rodin is great and Mirbeau is his prophet" This witticism dating from 1900 demonstrates the close friendship that had existed between Rodin and the journalist and novelist since the early 1880s. Octave Mirbeau was, in fact, one of the first art critics to defend the sculptor. The two exchanged voluminous correspondence – the museum has nearly 200 letters from Mirbeau to the sculptor – and, as a token of his recognition and friendship, the sculptor modelled the portrait bust of the man of letters in 1888.

Mirbeau, who had worked as a ghostwriter to pay off his debts from 1872 to 1884, could easily sympathize with Rodin who, until the age of 44, was also employed by other sculptors, including Carrier-Belleuse, who took credit for his works.

Rodin kept his promise to the writer, staying on two occasions on his estate near Laigle (Orne), where Mirbeau wrote two of his books, *Lettres de ma chaumière* and *Les Lettres de l'Inde*.

H. P.

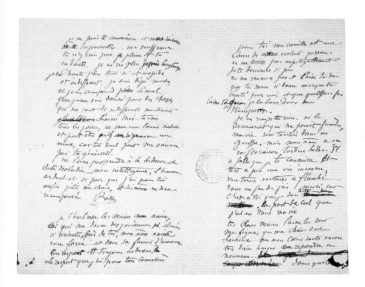

182

Letter from Auguste Rodin to Camille Claudel (1864-1943)

Circa 1886

Ink on paper
H. 21 cm; W. 27 cm
L. 1451

«Je t'embrasse les mains mon amie, toi qui me donnes des jouissances si élevées, si ardentes, près de toi, mon âme existe avec force et, dans sa fureur d'amour, ton respect est toujours au dessus. Le respect que j'ai pour ton caractère, pour toi ma Camille est une cause de ma violente passion. ne me traite pas impitoyablement je te demande si peu.»

"My ferocious friend". Thus begins Rodin's desperate cry of love to Camille Claudel in the early years of their relationship. Rodin was soon captivated by this pupil who became his assistant, mistress and muse, while Claudel outwardly remained in complete control of her feelings.

Consumed and tormented by an obsessive love, he implores her – "on his knees" – to ease his suffering from beginning to end of this letter, written in a muddled style, with erroneous syntax and imperfect spelling. It is a unique document in which Rodin, overwhelmed by his feelings, has no other choice but to open his heart sincerely and truthfully.

The rare documents in the museum archives – five letters from Rodin and about fifteen from Camille Claudel – often elated in tone, attest to this very intense and troubled relationship whose tragic ending is well known.

V. M.

In 1886, Claudel stayed with her friend Florence Jeans at her home in Shanklin, on the Isle of Wight. Two years later, the latter asked Camille and other friends to fill in the questionnaire, a very popular form of entertainment in certain circles of society on both sides of the Channel at this time, intended to reveal the personality of those who responded in an amusing manner. On this occasion, Camille Claudel was shown to have a strong character. Numerous celebrities, such as the French neurologist Professor Charcot (1825-93) and Claude Debussy (1862-1918), responded, but the questionnaire was named after a man of letters, Marcel Proust (1871-1922), who filled it in twice.

Camille Claudel was only 24 years old and the deliberately provocative, occasionally darkly ironic tone of her answers reflected a fiercely independent character, determined to be noticed. When asked, "Who are your favourite painters and composers?", she replied, "Myself." However, the significance of her replies should be put into perspective. The atmosphere was probably more conducive to having fun than being serious.

H. P.

183

Confessions. An Album to Record Opinions, Thoughts, Feelings, Ideas, Peculiarities, Impressions, Characteristics of Friends & c…

16 May 1888
H. 38.2 cm; W. 23.2 cm
Gift of Stephen Back, 1992
Ms. 368

184

Letter from Leopold von Sacher-Masoch (1836-1895) to Auguste Rodin

10 April 1887
Ink on paper
H. 17.8 cm; W. 22.3 cm
Ms. 777

Art critics and writers used to ask Rodin to let them attend posing sessions as a favour. The nude bodies of his models, and the occasionally ambiguous relationship between the sculptor and the young women, fed their own fantasies. Leopold von Sacher-Masoch, who was excited by one of these "magnificent tigresses", had acquired notoriety some years earlier with a semi-autobiographical novel called *Venus in Furs*, to which he alludes in this letter. It tells the story of a man dominated by a woman called Wanda, submitting to her every whim. Sacher-Masoch himself had this sort of relationship with his wife. In 1873, he drew up a contract similar in form to the one Rodin signed for Camille Claudel in 1886. But while Rodin promised his love to Camille alone and Sacher-Masoch pledged to be Wanda's slave, having given his wife his heroine's name, the writer sought a form of humiliation quite alien to Rodin's aspirations.

H. P.

« Cher Monsieur
je suis fier de votre amitié, car
elle me prouve que vous avez
trouvé dans mes œuvres un peu
de cette vérité et de cette force
élémentaire que j'ai tant
admirées dans tout ce que

j'ai vu de vous. J'ai rêvé
la nuit de vos magnifiques
tigresses humaines, et j'en
rêve encore les yeux ouverts en
plein jour. C'est un peu le
type de ma Vénus aux
fourrures que je ne puis
vous offrir malheureusement
car elle n'a pas paru en

français. Le marbre et le
bronze s'animent sous vos
doigts, comme la terre sous
le souffle de Dieu, le sixième
jour de la Création. Vous avez
donné à cette Matière Morte
ce qui lui manquait depuis
Phidias, le mouvement
et la vie.

Je vous serre la main
encore une fois et vous
dis de tout mon cœur
Au revoir

Sacher Masoch »

185

*Letter from Camille
Claudel to Auguste Rodin*

Summer 1890 or 1891(?)

Ink on paper
H. 17.5; W. 22 cm
Ms. 362

At the height of Rodin and Camille Claudel's relationship, there was a jealously guarded secret, a place where they used to meet whenever they visited Touraine: the Château de L'Islette. Situated just four kilometres from Azay-le-Rideau, they went there several times in 1890 and 1891. This was where they could enjoy being together and share the simple pleasures of everyday life. Protected by the castle towers, cut off from public life and official or social obligations, the two lovers savoured the time they spent peacefully in each other's company.

And if Rodin was sometimes compelled to leave her, Claudel knew which arguments to use to draw him back, as is shown in this touching letter that speaks of the tenderest moments of this relationship. Several upstairs rooms of the château were reserved for them, some of which served as a studio. Camille Claudel modelled the bust of *La Petite Châtelaine* here, while Rodin turned the largest room into the backdrop for the long posing sessions that he inflicted upon a driver working at Azay-le-Rideau, who just happened to be Balzac's double.

V. M.

186

Letter from Émile Zola (1840-1902) to Auguste Rodin

14 August 1891

Ink on paper
H. 21.5 cm; W. 27 cm
Ms. 776

In 1888, the Société des Gens de Lettres had commissioned a *Monument to Balzac* from the sculptor Henri Chapu (1833-91). However, the artist died before completing his sketch and, thanks to the influence of Émile Zola (1840-1902), appointed chairman of the society in 1892, Rodin was chosen to complete the project **(52)**.

Like the other members of the society, Zola wanted the monument to be finished by 1 May 1893 – the writer was then nearing the end of his novel *Doctor Pascal*, the last episode in the Rougeon-Macquart series. But Rodin, who was going through a difficult period in his life, worked much more slowly than hoped for. Despite the strained relationship that developed between the sculptor and his clients, Zola, whose role was also called into question by his peers, supported Rodin until the work was finally unveiled in 1898. That same year, in a virulent article entitled "J'accuse", published in the newspaper *L'Aurore*, Zola focused his attention on the defence of Captain Dreyfus.

H. P.

187

*Letter from Émile Antoine
Bourdelle (1861-1929)
to Auguste Rodin*

20 September 1893

Ink on paper
H. 13.6 cm; W. 18.1 cm
Not inventoried

After his exhibition in 1889 at the Galerie Georges Petit (1856-1920), Rodin recruited new assistants to help him meet an influx of commissions. François Pompon (1855-1933), Jean Escoula (1851-1911), Victor Peter (1840-1918) and Antoine Bourdelle thus joined the team working for him, of which Jules Desbois (1851-1935) had already been a part for several years. All of them led their own independent careers in tandem.

This letter from Bourdelle, written right at the beginning of their collaboration, conveys his enthusiasm and provides insight into his rela-

tionship wth Rodin. It took more than being a good sculptor to be a good assistant or practitioner; one also had to learn the master's style. When he wrote this letter, Bourdelle was busy carving a marble commissioned by a patron. Having reached an advanced stage in his work, he asked Rodin for his opinion before finishing it.

The two artists remained on good terms, even after Bourdelle stopped working for Rodin. They shared the same love of Greco-Roman antiquities which they both collected.

H. P.

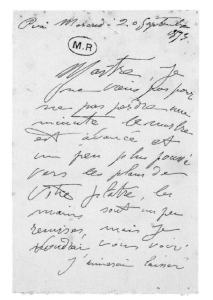 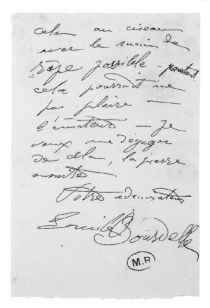

188

*Letter from Auguste Rodin
to Claude Monet
(1840-1926)*

22 September 1897

Ink on paper
H. 14 cm; W. 26.1 cm
Acquired in 2007
L. 1707

Rodin and Monet's friendship is known to have existed even before the famous exhibition in 1889 to promote the two leading artists of the day.

At the time, Rodin was feeling extremely vulnerable, shaken both by the break-up of his relationship with Camille Claudel and the repeated complaints from the Société des Gens de Lettres, who had commissioned the *Monument to Balzac* (52) and whose impatience was exacerbated by years of waiting.

In the face of this general lack of understanding, Rodin again found support from his admirers and loyal friends.

This letter, acquired in 2006, reveals the artistic rapport and the friendship that united the two men. It is moving testimony to the sculptor's admiration for the painter and his oeuvre, a feeling that Rodin seldom – perhaps never – expressed so clearly or so elegantly: "the same feeling of fraternity, the same love of art, has made us friends for ever… I still have the same admiration for the artist who helped me understand light, clouds, the sea, the Cathedrals that I already loved so much, but whose beauty awakened at dawn by your rendering touched me so deeply."

V. M.

189

Letter from Auguste Rodin to Helene von Hindenburg (1878-1944)

22 November 1902

Ink on paper
H. 17.8 cm; W. 11.2 cm
Acquired in 1960
L. 764

In 1900, the young German aristocrat, Helene von Hindenbourg, was just 22 when she was introduced to Rodin, then at the height of his fame. Meeting him made a strong impression on her and marked the beginning of a long friendship, kept up by an abundant and quite extraordinary correspondence.

In 1901 and 1902, Rodin stayed at her villa in Ardenza, Italy, where they shared moments of intense artistic sensibility which the sculptor never forgot. Together they explored the region, marvelling at its much-coveted treasures. Evenings were reserved for reading and music, and in a quasi-mystical atmosphere, she played Beethoven for him on the piano.

In the letters they exchanged, they talked endlessly of the Antique and the Renaissance, praising Perugino, writing enthusiastically about Michelangelo and sharing their musical preferences. In an unusually careful epistolary style, Rodin expressed his innermost emotions, at the same time revealing a rare fervour.

V. M.

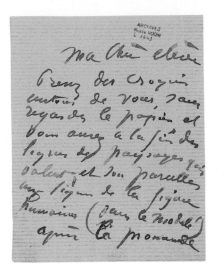

190

Letter from Auguste Rodin to Sophie Postolska (1868-1943)

Undated
Ink on paper
H. 13.2 cm; W. 20.7 cm
Acquired in 2005
L. 1649

Sophie Postolska, Rodin's Polish-born model, pupil and mistress, was the sister-in-law of Louis Dorizon, chairman of the bank Société Générale, who, together with Joanny Peytel and Albert Kahn, financed Rodin's exhibition at the Pavillon de l'Alma in 1900.

The sculptor is known to have had a prolific sentimental life, which developed at the same pace as his fame. A stream of models, pupils and women of the world came to his studio to seduce this great sculptor of women who, because he desired them, could study them like a clinician. Sophie Postolska was one of them, but the letter Rodin writes here is addressed to the pupil and provides valuable evidence of the sculptor's teaching methods. He insisted on the importance of practising drawing, recommending that each of his pupils make sketches as if taking notes, so as to train the eye and hand to jot lines down rapidly, the sole purpose of which was to capture fleeting, much-coveted truth.

V. M.

«Ma chère élève

*Prenez des croquis
autour de vous, sans
regarder le papier et
vous aurez à la fin des
lignes de paysages qui
valent et son (sic) pareilles
aux lignes de la figure
humaine (sans le modelé)
après la promenade*

*faites, cela rapidement
en 3 minutes et par
conséquent en grand
nombre. Dessinez puisque
vous ne pouvez modeler
    J'envi (sic) votre jeunesse
Votre force devant les
merveilles que vous
voyez, et que par l'étude
vous vous assimilerez.
C'est le bonheur véritable
et très doux qui*

*récompense le travailleur
à tous les âges de la vie
mais surtout à celui que j'ai
quand les Dieux sont partis
et que l'on reste dépouillé.
J'ai néanmoins des amis et
leur affection m'est chère
et cela est ma ligne d'horizon
Avec mes affectueux sentiments
            Rodin»*

191

Letter from Rainer Maria Rilke (1875-1926) to Auguste Rodin

31 August 1908

Ink on paper
H. 18.2 cm; W. 13.7 cm
Ms. 484

This fine letter from one of the greatest German poets was the starting point of Rodin's relationship with the Hôtel Biron, which would lead to the founding of the museum, in 1916.

Rainer Maria Rilke was not yet 30 when he met Rodin in 1902. From the outset, he devoted himself to the man who had just been proclaimed the latest master sculptor. Rodin's genius, combined with his rare capacity for work and instinctive originality, so fascinated Rilke that he made him his mentor. He constantly sought to translate Rodin's poetic creations into words.

In 1905, so as to help the writer financially, Rodin invited him to stay at Meudon in exchange for some secretarial work, before abruptly dismissing him eight months later. Deeply hurt by Rodin's overly cantankerous attitude towards him, Rilke nevertheless remained attached to the sculptor's oeuvre, while his "intellectual admiration" fortunately prompted him to forget this misunderstanding.

It was Rilke who happened to find the Hôtel Biron, then divided into rented apartments, in 1908. He moved in and immediately told Rodin how charming it was.

A few weeks later, Rodin installed his studio there for the rest of his life.

V. M.

Letters from abroad

From the 1890s onwards, Rodin's immense fame was reflected in the letters he received from abroad. These selected examples highlight the diversity of his correspondents and depict a busy international social life.

For example, he enjoyed a long friendship with the Norwegian painter Fritz Thaulow (1847-1906), who gave him several pictures. The English sculptor John Tweed (1869-1933) wanted Rodin's opinion on his work modelled from life; the American dancers Isadora Duncan (1878-1927) and Loie Fuller (1862-1928) begged him to come to their Parisian shows. During one of Rodin's many visits to London, the American painter John Singer Sargent (1856-1925) invited him to have lunch with him. Alfred Stieglitz (1864-1946) thanked him warmly for the loan of his drawings exhibited in his New York Gallery 291, while, in 1906, the German collector August Thyssen (1842-1926) enquired anxiously about the three marbles he had commissioned from Rodin – *The Death of Athens, Young Girl Confiding her Secret to a Shade, Christ and the Magdalen* (**43**), which had to be sent to him by train.

H. P.

192

Visiting card from John Singer Sargent to Rodin
Undated
Ink on paper
H. 3.8 cm; W. 7.6 cm

Printed invitation: *"Danses-Idylles de Miss Isadora Duncan, 45, avenue de Villiers, Friday evening, 31 May – 9 o'clock"*
H. 13.8 cm; W. 22 cm

Telegram from Fritz Thaulow to Rodin
15 May 1901
Ink on paper
H. 14.5 cm; W. 11.3 cm

Letter from August Thyssen to Rodin
27 January 1906
Ink on paper
H. 21.9 cm; W. 28.4 cm

Letter from John Tweed to Rodin
Early 1905
Ink on paper
H. 20.5; W. 15.4 cm

Letter from Alfred Stieglitz to Rodin
17 January 1908
Ink on paper
H. 22.3 cm; W. 33.4 cm

Telegram from Loie Fuller to Rodin
14 September 1898
H. 18 cm; W. 23.5 cm

193

Notebooks
and Sketchbooks
of Auguste Rodin

Ink and lead pencil on paper

Notes and rough sketches

Among the thousands of autograph documents hoarded by Rodin, and shedding light on his life, are several hundred notebooks and all sorts of rough sketches which, although part of the donation the sculptor made to the French state in 1916, remain little known.

With his dubious spelling, erroneous syntax and often illegible writing, Rodin became accustomed to filling up these notebooks, in all shapes and sizes. In them, he jotted down a stream of unrelated ideas, as if to help him remember an impression, a feeling or emotion, rather like an *aide-mémoire*, and could either take the form of a drawing or a hastily scribbled sketch.

It is hard to find a use for these notes which were never dated, and yet they form an essential link with the artist's everyday life, prerequisite to understanding the sculptor. Above all, they provide a very rare opportunity to gain insight into his innermost thoughts.

V. M.

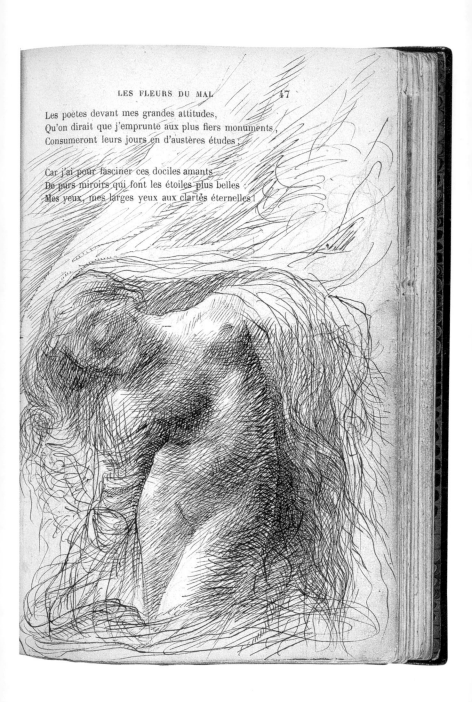

LES FLEURS DU MAL   47

Les poètes devant mes grandes attitudes,
Qu'on dirait que j'emprunte aux plus fiers monuments,
Consumeront leurs jours en d'austères études ;

Car j'ai pour fasciner ces dociles amants
De purs miroirs qui font les étoiles plus belles :
Mes yeux, mes larges yeux aux clartés éternelles !

194

CHARLES BAUDELAIRE

Les Fleurs du Mal
(The Flowers of Evil)

**Paris, Poulet-Malassis
and De Broise, 1857**

H.18.7 cm; W. 12 cm
Acquired in 1931
D. 7174

This copy of the original edition of 1857 belonged to the book lover Paul Gallimard. The architect and art critic Frantz Jourdain used his influence to obtain the commission to illustrate it for Rodin. The brown leather binding was made by Henri Marius Michel. Represented in demi-relief on the front cover, in incised, mosaiced leather, is an ivory skull on a dark green thistle plant.

Rodin, whose fondness for poetry and Baudelaire is well known, worked on this project for barely four months, in late 1887 and early 1888. His line drawings, sometimes heavily shaded, with hatched backgrounds and five washes on Japan paper, heavy with ink and gouache, would subsequently be inserted into the pages. Specially designed for the book or inspired by earlier sketches made for *The Gates of Hell*, these drawings appeared on the frontispiece and occasionally invaded the poems.

This unique copy was acquired by the Musée Rodin in 1931 through Messrs David Weill and Maurice Fenaille.

V. M.

195

OCTAVE MIRBEAU

*Le Jardin des Supplices
(The Torture Garden),*

Paris, Ambroise Vollard, 1902

H. 32.7 cm; W. 25.5 cm

Inv. 6730

Lithograph by Auguste Clot.

Amongst Rodin's limited work as an illustrator, his collaboration with his loyal friend and fervent champion, Octave Mirbeau (1848-1917), on the latter's book *The Torture Garden*, sealed their friendship for ever. In 1889, the two men, bound by the same aesthetic struggle against sterile academicism, formed a very united group with Monet and the art critic Gustave Geffroy.

In 1899, after a somewhat modest first edition, Rodin and Mirbeau signed a contract with the picture dealer Ambroise Vollard, for the illustration of a luxury edition of Mirbeau's novel, *The Torture Garden*. The book was published in 1902, illustrated with 20 lithographs, protected by tissue guards, accompanied by captions and line engravings. Most of the prints of the drawings were made by the lithographer Auguste Clot (1858-1936).

Rodin's imagination was fired by the skilful mix of sinister violence and voluptuousness in this novel. He concentrated almost exclusively on the heroine Clara and the theme of Sapphic love, which is known to have been a source of inspiration for the artist's drawings.

V. M.

196

Les Cathédrales de France
by Auguste Rodin
Éditions Armand Colin, 1914
Inv. 6756

In *L'Art*, published in 1911 by Grasset, Rodin replied at length to the journalist Paul Gsell's questions. But it was another kind of book that the writer Charles Morice (1861-1919) decided to work on shortly after 1910. He began by compiling the notes that Rodin had jotted down about cathedrals in the course of his numerous journeys across France. The writer was a good friend of the artist. In 1900, he had given a series lectures and written a book about Rodin's art. He therefore did not content himself with just writing a long preface, but probably rewrote passages of the sculptor's prose. Rodin must have found it hard to accept these amendments, judging from the writer's reply: "Wasn't it precisely because I was going to put your thoughts into a suitable form that you considered my collaboration useful?"

H. P.

Plate XXVIII. Dijon Cathedral.

197

VLADIMIR ŽUPANSKÝ (1869-1928)

Poster of the Rodin Exhibition in Prague

10 May-15 July 1902

H. 158 cm; W. 84 cm

Af. 172

In May 1902, the Manès Union of Artists, Prague, hosted an exhibition of Rodin's works in the pavilion built in 1901 by one of its members, Jan Kotěra (1871-1923). A pupil of the Viennese architect, Otto Wagner, Kotěra had also mounted the exhibition, following Rodin's written instructions. The project had commenced in 1898.

Rodin, who had had to attend a dinner given in his honour in London, arrived in Prague via Cologne and Dresden, after the official opening. He was accompanied by his favourite pupil, the sculptor Joseph Mařatka (1874-1937), the painter Alfons Mucha (1860-1939) and Rudolph Vácha (born 1860). On 30 May, a banquet was held for him in Prague.

The exhibition, for which a catalogue was published, was advertised by a poster – one of the rare posters to have survived from Rodin's period – depicting his *Balzac* (1898). Designed by the painter and poster artist Vladimir Županský, its style is characteristic of the Art Nouveau aesthetics prevalent in Vienna, Prague and Berlin at this time.

Rodin's work was widely known and shown in Germany and Central Europe, before, but especially after, his major retrospective of 1900, owing to the exhibitions organized by artists belonging to the *Sezession* movement, for whom Rodin epitomized modernity in sculpture.

H. P.

— Ceci m'a été inspiré par un poème de M. Jean Rameau.

198

Caricature of Rodin
by Paul Iribe (1883-1935),
published in *L'Assiette au beurre*,
on 25 April 1903

Rodin and his works, especially *The Thinker* (68), were frequently caricatured in the press. *L'Assiette au beurre*, one of the most famous satirical reviews of the day, ran from 1901 to 1912 and published virulent anticlerical, antimilitarist and anticapitalist caricatures. Paul Iribe was one the regular contributors to the review, together with Jean-Louis Forain (1852-1931), Félix Valloton (1865-1925) and Charles Léandre (1862-1943), to name those whose pens poked fun at Rodin. They all worked on other Parisian newspapers like *Le Cri de Paris* and *Le Rire*.

This drawing refers to Jean Rameau (1852-1931), the "poet/clog-maker" as he described himself, who was best known as a writer of French folksongs, the words of which were printed on postcards and thus circulated without difficulty.

H. P.

ANNEXES

Selected Bibliography

Ruth BUTLER, *Rodin: The Shape of Genius,* New Haven and London, Yale University Press, 1993.

Catherine CHEVILLOT (dir.), *Le musée de Rodin. Dernier chef-d'œuvre du sculpteur,* Paris, Éditions du musée Rodin / Artlys, 2015.

Catherine CHEVILLOT, *Rodin. L'invention permanente,* Paris, Gallimard / Rmn – Grand Palais, coll. "Hors série. Découvertes", 2017.

Albert E. ELSEN, *Rodin Rediscovered,* Washington, D.C., National Gallery of Art, 1981.

Rosalind E. KRAUSS, *Passages in Modern Sculpture,* Cambridge, Mass., The MIT Press, 1977.

Frederic V. GRUNFELD, *Rodin, A Biography,* New York, Henry Holt and Co., 1987.

Antoinette LE NORMAND-ROMAIN, *Rodin,* Paris, Éditions Citadelles & Mazenod, 2013.

Antoinette LE NORMAND-ROMAIN, *The Bronzes of Rodin. Catalogue of Works in the Musée Rodin,* Paris, Éditions du Musée Rodin / Réunion des Musées Nationaux, 2007, two-volume set.

Antoinette LE NORMAND-ROMAIN, Christina BULEY-URIBE, *Drawings and Watercolours,* Paris, Hazan, 2006.

Nadine LEHNI, *Rodin, son musée secret,* Paris, Éditions du musée Rodin / Albin Michel, 2017.

Aline MAGNIEN, *Rodin and Eroticism,* Paris, Éditions du musée Rodin / Hermann, 2016.

Raphaël MASSON, Véronique MATTIUSSI, *Rodin,* Paris, Éditions du Musée Rodin / Flammarion, 2004.

Rainer Maria RILKE, *Auguste Rodin,* London, Pallas Athene, 2007.

Auguste RODIN, *Rodin on Art and Artists,* New York, Dover Publications, 2009.

Exhibition catalogues
In chronological order

Nadine LEHNI, Marie-Thérèse PULVÉNIS DE SELIGNY (dir.), *Matisse & Rodin,* Paris, Éditions du musée Rodin/Rmn, 2009.

François BLANCHETIÈRE, William SAADÉ (dir.), *Rodin. Les arts décoratifs,* Paris, Éditions du musée Rodin / Alternatives, 2010.

Hélène PINET, Anita FELDMAN (dir.), *Henry Moore. L'Atelier,* Paris, Éditions du musée Rodin/Hazan, 2010.

Dominique VIÉVILLE, Aline MAGNIEN (dir.), *L'Invention de l'œuvre. Rodin & les ambassadeurs,* Paris, Éditions du musée Rodin/Actes Sud, 2011.

Dominique VIÉVILLE, Nadine LEHNI (dir.), *La Saisie du modèle. Rodin. 300 dessins (1890-1917),* Paris, Éditions du musée Rodin/Nicolas Chaudun, 2011.

Aline MAGNIEN (dir.), *Rodin, la chair, le marbre,* Paris, Éditions du musée Rodin/Hazan, 2012.

Pascale PICARD, Bénédicte GARNIER (dir.), *Rodin, la lumière de l'Antique,* Paris, Gallimard, 2013.

Hélène PINET, Hélène MARRAUD, Judith BENHAMOU-HUET (dir.), *Mapplethorpe/Rodin,* Paris, Éditions du musée Rodin/Actes Sud, 2014.

François BLANCHETIERE (dir.), *L'Enfer selon Rodin,* Paris, Éditions du musée Rodin / Norma, 2016.

Catherine CHEVILLOT, Véronique MATTIUSSI, Sylvie PATRY (dir.), *Kiefer Rodin,* Paris, Éditions du musée Rodin / Gallimard / The Barnes Foundation, 2017.

Catherine CHEVILLOT, Antoinette LE NORMAND-ROMAIN (dir.), *Rodin. Le livre du centenaire,* Paris, Rmn – Grand Palais, 2017.

Bibliography

ANONYMOUS
[1892-1] "Le Monument de
Baudelaire. Baudelaire traduit
par Rodin," Paris, 22 Sept.
1892
[1892-2] "Au jour le jour.
Le monument de Charles
Baudelaire," *Le Temps*,
27 Sept. 1892

BENJAMIN René [1910]
"Les dessins d'Auguste
Rodin," *Gil Blas*,
17 Oct.-8 Nov. 1910

BULEY-URIBE Christina
[2006]
"The ultimate point
of his work" in Antoinette
Le Normand-Romain
and Christina Buley-Uribe,
*Auguste Rodin, Drawings
& Watercolours*, Paris, Hazan,
2006, p. 34

CANUDO Ricciotto [1913]
"Une visite à Rodin," *Revue
hebdomadaire*, 5 Apr. 1913

CLADEL Judith [1936]
*Rodin, sa vie glorieuse, sa vie
inconnue*, Paris, Grasset, 1936,
pp. 109, 275

CLAUDEL Paul [1951]
Camille Claudel, exhibition
catalogue, Musée Rodin,
Nov.-Dec. 1951, Paris,
Éditions du Musée Rodin,
1951, p. 3

DES CARS Laurence [2007]
Gustave Courbet, exhibition
catalogue, Galeries Nationales
du Grand Palais, 13 Oct.
2007-28 Jan. 2008, Paris,

Éditions de la Réunion
des Musées Nationaux, 2007,
p. 382

DUJARDIN-BEAUMETZ
Henri [1913]
Entretiens avec Rodin, Paris,
1913, pp. 65, 111. Reprinted
by the Éditions du Musée
Rodin in 1992.

GSELL Paul [1911]
*Auguste Rodin, L'Art.
Entretiens avec Paul Gsell*,
Paris, 1911

GUENNE Jacques [1925]
Matisse interviewed by
Jacques Guenne, *L'Art vivant*,
15 Sept. 1925

JUDRIN Claudie
[1992]
Inventaire des dessins, vol. V,
Paris, published by the Musée
Rodin, 1992, p. 72
[2002]
Hell and Paradise, Paris,
published by the Musée
Rodin, coll. "Tout l'œuvre",
2002, p. 65

PIERRON Sander [1935]
"Auguste Rodin, peintre du
Brabant," in *Le Flambeau*,
Brussels, no. 7, July 1935, p. 72

PINET Hélène [2007]
Rodin et la photographie,
exhibition catalogue, Musée
Rodin, 14 Nov. 2007-2 Mar.
2008, Paris,
Gallimard/Éditions du Musée
Rodin, 2007, p. 29

REVERS Henry [1911]
"Chez Auguste Rodin", in
Les Nouvelles, 30-31 Dec. 1911

RILKE Rainer Maria
[1905]
Letter to Clara Rilke,
20 Sept. 1905, in Rainer
Maria Rilke, *Œuvres 3.
Correspondance*, Paris,
Éditions du Seuil, 1976
[1908]
Letter to Auguste Rodin,
31 Aug. 1908, Paris,
Musée Rodin archives
[1928]
Auguste Rodin, Paris, 1928,
pp. 52-53, 112

RODIN Auguste
[1893]
Letter to Omer Dewavrin,
8 Dec. 1893, Calais,
municipal archives
[1904]
"La tête Warren", *Le Musée*,
Nov.-Dec. 1904, pp. 298-301
[1909]
Rodin quoted in "Van
Gogh", in *Le Cri de Paris*,
14 Nov. 1909
[1914]
Les Cathédrales de France, Paris,
Armand Collin, 1914, p. 39
[1943]
Le Panorama, 21 Oct. 1943

TIREL Marcelle [1923]
*Rodin intime ou l'envers
d'une gloire*, Paris, Éditions
du Monde Nouveau, 1923,
pp. 14, 50

VARNEDOE Kirk [1971]
The Drawings of Rodin,
New-York, 1971, pp. 87-92

Index of works

Entries in this guide are indicated by boldface page numbers

The works are fragile. Please do not touch them. Using a mobile phone, smoking, eating and drinking inside the exhibition spaces are forbidden. Visitors are not allowed to walk on the grass or picnic in the gardens. Photographs taken without a flash are permitted in the Hôtel Biron, but unauthorized in temporary exhibitions.

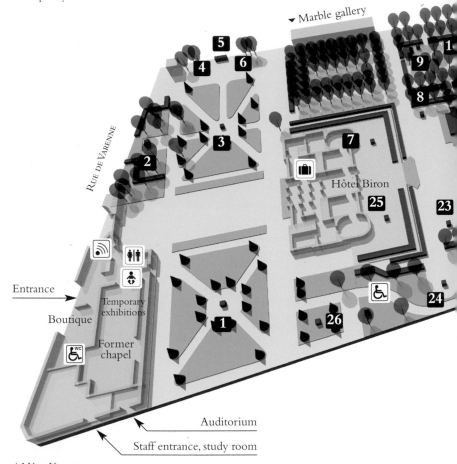

Marble gallery

5

4 6

RUE DE VARENNE

3

2

Hôtel Biron

7

25

23

1

9

8

Entrance

Temporary exhibitions

Boutique

Former chapel

1

26

24

Auditorium

Staff entrance, study room

◀ Métro Varenne
◀ RER Invalides

Plan of the Musée Rodin

Designed by Vincent Lecocq

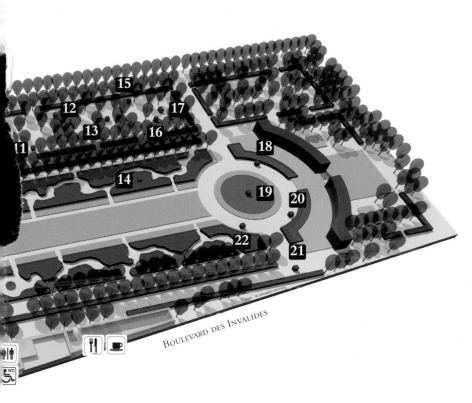

1. The Thinker **(68)**
2. The Burghers of Calais **(25-plaster version)**
3. The Three Shades **(30)**
4. Adam **(15)**
5. The Gates of Hell **(14)**
6. Eve **(16)**
7. Cybele
8. Fallen Caryatid carrying her Stone
9. Studies for Pierre de Wissant
10. Eustache de Saint Pierre
11. Jean de Fiennes
12. Jules Bastien-Lepage
13. Andreu d'Andres
14. Orpheus
15. Jacques de Wissant
16. Jean d'Aire
17. Monument to Victor Hugo **(39)**
18. The Shade
19. Ugolino **(17-plaster version)**
20. The Spirit of Eternal Repose
21. Claude Lorrain
22. Meditation
23. Fallen Caryatid with Urn
24. Aphrodite
25. The Whistler Muse **(79)**
26. Monument to Balzac **(52)**

Photographic credits

© musée Rodin, Paris: p. 8, 10, 11, 12, 14, 15, 169, 180, 182, 183, 184, 185, 186, 187, 188, 189, 190, 191, 192, 193, 194, 195, 196, 197, 198, 199, 200, 201, 202, 226, 227, 230, 232, 233, 234, 236, 237, 243

© musée Rodin, photo Christian Baraja: front cover, p. 18, 21, 22, 24, 25, 26-27, 28-29, 32, 43, 51, 53, 58, 60, 61, 62, 66, 67, 68, 70, 71, 74, 76, 77, 78, 80, 81, 82, 83, 85, 89, 92, 96, 97, 99, 100, 101, 105, 107, 110, 111, 113, 114-115, 116, 117, 131, 170, 171, 211, 235, 238

© musée Rodin, photo Jean de Calan: p. 23, 37, 38, 39, 95, 106, 118, 167, 175, 178, 122, 123, 124, 126, 128, 129, 131, 132, 133, 134, 136, 137, 139, 140, 142, 143, 144, 147, 148, 149, 151, 223, 224, 239, 240, 241

© musée Rodin, photo Béatrice Hatala: p. 34, 35, 42, 47, 49, 54, 57, 73, 87, 125, 176, 216, 218, 220, 222, 243

© musée Rodin, photo Erik & Petra Hesmerg: p. 79

© musée Rodin, photo Bruno Jarret: p. 130, 172, 173, 179, 145

© musée Rodin, photo Luc Joubert: p. 214

© musée Rodin, photo Luc & Lala Joubert: p. 210, 213, 215, 221

© musée Rodin, photo Jérôme Manoukian: p. 4, 228, 229, 231

© musée Rodin, photo Adam Rzepka: p. 30, 31, 33, 36, 40-41, 45, 48, 50, 52, 55, 56, 63, 64, 69, 88, 90, 103, 109, 116, 150, 154, 157, 158, 159, 168, 204, 205, 206, 207, 208, 209, 212, 217, 219, 242, 245, 246

© musée Rodin, photo Philippe Sebert: p. 177

© musée Rodin/ADAGP, photo Christian Baraja: p. 160-161, 162, 163, 164-165, 166
© musée Rodin/ADAGP, photo Jean de Calan: p. 65, 121
© musée Rodin/ADAGP, photo Erik & Petra Hesmerg: p. 98
© musée Rodin/ADAGP, photo Bruno Jarret: p.141
© musée Rodin/ADAGP, photo Adam Rzepka: p. 46, 64, 72, 84, 86, 91, 93, 94, 102, 104, 108, 112, 127, 138

© The Estate of Edward Steichen: p. 190, 191, 192, 200

Printed in July 2018
in Spain by Fabrikant

Registration of copyright: July 2018
1st edition: 2008
ISBN: 978-2-35377-009-0
ISBN French edition: 978-2-35377-008-3